# JEREMIAH'S
# POEMS
# OF LAMENT

## Walter Baumgartner

Translated by
David E. Orton

The Almond  Press · 1988

Translated by David E. Orton
Edited by David M. Gunn

Copyright © 1987 Sheffield Academic Press

Published by Almond Press
Editorial direction: David M. Gunn
Columbia Theological Seminary
P.O. Box 520, Decatur
GA 30031, U.S.A.
Almond Press is an imprint of
Sheffield Academic Press Ltd
The University of Sheffield
343 Fulwood Road
Sheffield S10 3BP
England

Typeset by Sheffield Academic Press
and
printed in Great Britain
by Billing & Sons Ltd
Worcester

British Library Cataloguing in Publication Data

Baumgartner, Walter
    Jeremiah's Poems of Lament.—(Historic
    texts and interpreters in biblical
    scholarship, ISSN 0263-1199; 7).
    1. Bible. O.T. Jeremiah—Criticism,
    interpretation, etc.
    I. Title                        II. Series
    224.'.206                       BS1525.2

    ISBN 1-85075-116-1
    ISBN 1-85075-115-3 Pbk

## CONTENTS

Chapter 4
THE RELATIONSHIP OF JEREMIAH'S POEMS OF LAMENT TO THE SONGS OF LAMENT TYPE 79
1. The authenticity of the Poems of Lament in Jeremiah 79
a. The prophetic element of the Poems of Lament 80
b. The relation of the form and content of the Poems of Lament to the Songs of Jeremiah that are acknowledged as genuine 82
c. The Communal Song of Lament in Jeremiah 88
2. The dependence of Jeremiah's Poems of Lament on the Songs of Lament type 89
a. The greater antiquity of the type 89
b. The adoption of the type by Jeremiah 95
c. Jeremiah's poetic individuality 99

Notes 103
Index to prophetic passages discussed 115

*Translator's Note*

Some of the terms used for literary classification in German works of this period have now become more or less technical terms, often left untranslated in English texts and italicized in German texts. In order both to preserve some flavour of the original, however, and to keep the translation as English as possible, these terms have been translated in the present text. The major terms in question, for which readers may be interested to know the corresponding German term, are as follows: 'type', or 'literary type', represents *Gattung*; 'setting in life' represents *Sitz im Leben*; 'poems of lament' represents *Klagegedichte*; 'songs of lament' represents *Klagelieder*; 'psalms of lament' represents *Klagepsalmen*; 'lament' represents *Klage*; 'petition' represents *Bitte*; 'assurance of being heard' represents *Gewißheit der Erhörung*.

Titles of cited scholarly works are translated in parentheses, except where the meaning is obvious. Where biblical references in the German original (which generally correspond to the Hebrew text) diverge from English versions, the English reference is supplied in parentheses. Some errors in the German references have been eliminated. For ease of reference to citations of the German original, the page numbers of that edition are marked in square brackets in the text.

Biblical quotations generally follow the RSV except where the author's own translation differs from it in his understanding of the Hebrew. It is, unfortunately, inevitable that poetic considerations have had to take second place.

D.E. Orton

## PREFACE

The question of the relationship of the 'poems of lament', 'psalms' or 'confessions' of Jeremiah to the songs of the Psalter and the book of Job played a part a few years ago in the passage of arms between Cornill and Sellin, when it could already look back on a long and varied history. It has since attracted renewed attention in the wake of the solution proposed by Hölscher. No special justification would seem necessary, therefore, for making it the subject of an investigation of our own.

A few comments on the structure of this work may be in order. The treatment of the songs of lament in Chapter 2 is only as detailed as I felt was warranted for the understanding of the text as a whole and its context. No definitive account of this literary type can be written until all the songs that belong to the type outside the Psalter have been treated. Nor is Chapter 3 intended to provide a comprehensive commentary, in all respects, on the relevant sections of the book of Jeremiah. Finally, the fact that in the same chapter only a limited number of songs are treated as 'poems of lament' is justified in that research has begun precisely with these and particular labels have already become established for these same songs. That they do not differ fundamentally from all the other sections of the book of Jeremiah, but simply emphasize more strongly and clearly certain features that are also found in other songs, is shown in Chapter 4.

I have made as thorough use as possible of the relevant literature to which I had access. My thanks are here expressed for all the kind help given to me personally. Professor P. Jensen in Marburg was kind enough to read through the section on the Assyrian psalms. Professor L. Köhler in Zürich placed at my disposal his thorough expertise in the Septuagint. To Professor K. Budde in Marburg I owe a series of valuable individual comments and corrections. My greatest thanks, however, are due to Professor H. Gunkel in Giessen, who for many years has greatly stimulated me by his books and lectures and above all in personal conversations, and who, in connection with this work too, has supported me time and again with his advice.

# ABBREVIATIONS

| | |
|---|---|
| *BH* | *Biblia hebraica*, ed. R. Kittel |
| G | Septuagint |
| MT | Masoretic Text |
| *NKZ* | *Neue kirchliche Zeitschrift* |
| *PRE*[3] | Herzog's *Realencyclopädie für prot. Theologie und Kirche*, third edition by Hauck |
| *RGG* | *Religion in Geschichte und Gegenwart* |
| S | Vetus Testamentum Syriacum, ed. Lee (1823) |
| T | Targum |
| *ThStKr* | *Theologische Studien und Kritiken* |
| V | Vulgate |
| *ZAW* | *Zeitschrift für die alttestamentliche Wissenschaft* |

# Chapter 1

# THE HISTORY OF THE QUESTION

It has long been recognized that certain parts of the book of Jeremiah—for the sake of simplicity I leave the book of Job out of consideration here—have quite close points of contact with a number of songs in the Psalter. Various attempts have been made to account for this phenomenon.

Since many of the psalms that most clearly reveal such a relationship, such as Pss. 31, 35, 40 and 69, are attributed to David, the most obvious assumption was that Jeremiah, being the more recent, imitated Davidic psalms. Such was the judgment of e.g. Aug. Kueper, *Jeremias librorum sacrorum interpres atque vindex* (1837), pp. 158-64; E.W. Hengstenberg, *Commentar über die Psalmen II* (1843), pp. 179f.; Frz Delitzsch, *Commentar über den Psalter* (3rd edn, 1873), p. 266; C.F. Keil, *Biblischer Kommentar über den Propheten Jeremia* (1878), p. 235; more recently C. von Orelli, *Der Prophet Jeremia* (3rd edn, 1905) on 18.20 and 20.11-13, and—not, however, maintaining the Davidic authorship of the Psalms—E. Sellin, *Disputatio de origine carminum, quae primus psalterii liber continet* (1892), pp. 118-22.

In the case of anonymous psalms, however, and where researchers no longer felt bound by the superscriptions to the psalms, that similarity led rather to the conclusion that the psalms in question derived from the pen of Jeremiah. The idea that Jeremiah authored psalms is, after all, an old one. Certain Septuagint MSS attribute Pss. 65, 137 and 138 to Jeremiah as well as David (cf. also some Vulgate MSS of Pss. 65 and 137), but this can hardly be due to simple observation of the texts (especially Pss. 65 and 137), which offer no obvious indication of such authorship. One might more plausibly draw on this idea to explain why Theodore of Mopsuestia deems Ps. 35 to have been spoken by David in Jeremiah's | [2] name.[1] In the seventeenth century an English theologian, Dean Jackson (1579-1640), expressed the opinion that a number of 'Davidic' psalms were composed by Jeremiah at the time of the Babylonian captivity.[2] The scholar, however, who actually justified this opinion on the basis of the mutual contacts and defended it in detail, was Ferd. Hitzig. In his *Psalmencommentar* of 1863-1865 he maintained, departing somewhat from his earlier 'Untersuchungen zu den Psalmen' [Investigations in the Psalms] (1835), that Pss. 5, 6, 22, 28, 30, 31, 35, 38, 40, 55 and 69-71 were certainly composed by Jeremiah and Pss. 14, 23-27, 29, 32-34, 37, 39, 41 and 53 possibly so. With regard to Ps. 31 he was followed by H. Ewald, *Die Psalmen* (2nd edn, 1840), p. 173, and later by Fr. W. Schultz and H. Strack in their *Psalmenkommentar* (1888), p. 78. H. Hupfeld's view was that Hitzig's instinct was correct when he attributed a number of psalms to Jeremiah, something which was in fact very likely to be the case, even if Hitzig did frequently try to prove it in the wrong place or in an inappropriate way (*Die Psalmen* [1855], IV, p. 467 = [2nd edn, 1868], I, p. 50). A similar view was expressed by De Wette, *Commentar über die Psalmen* (4th edn, 1836), p. 257, who, though he rejected the Jeremianic authorship of Pss. 22 and 31, otherwise thought it very probable 'that many psalms of lament derive from the long-suffering Jeremiah'. Steiner assumed that Jeremiah had penned Pss. 22, 30, 31, 35, 40, 69 and 71, and deemed others to have emanated from Jeremiah's circle (Schenkel's *Bibellexikon*, V [1875], p. 5). Indeed even Frz Delitzsch adopted Hitzig's suggestion in respect of Pss. 40, 69 and 71. The most recent representative of this view seems to be C.J. Ball, who in his *Jeremiah* (1890), pp. 10f., with reference to Hitzig, derives Pss. 23 and 26-28 from Jeremiah.[3]

With the recognition that the Psalter was the hymn-book of the Second Temple and the great majority of its songs a product of the post-exilic period, these two attempted explanations had to be abandoned. Psalms of Jeremiah had become just as improbable as Psalms of David. Whenever those contacts were investigated at all, priority was now ascribed to the prophet, who had been an example to the later psalmists in his suffering and in the way he expressed it: thus. Fr. Baethgen, *Die Psalmen* (2nd edn, 1904), p. 86; Ch. A. Briggs, *The Book of Psalms* I (1907), p. 264; Fr. Buhl, *PRE*, VIII, p. 660; T.K. Cheyne, *The Origin and Religious Contents of the Psalter* (1891), pp. 122, 135f., with an express | [3] refutation of Hitzig; C.H. Cornill, *Das Buch Jeremia* (1905), p. 151; S.R. Driver, *The Book of the Prophet Jeremiah* (1906), p. 118; Fr. Giesebrecht, *Jeremiah* (2nd edn, 1907), p. 135; E. Kautzsch, *Die Heilige Schrift des A.T.* II (3rd edn, 1910), p. 137; J. Olshausen, *Die Psalmen* (1853), p. 146; J. Smend, *Lehrbuch der alttestamentlichen Religionsgeschichte* (2nd edn, 1899), p. 264; J. Wellhausen, *The Book of Psalms* (1898), p. 178.

To be sure, only a few of those named, Buhl, Cheyne, Smend and Wellhausen, make a comprehensive statement on the matter. Usually a judgment is given in respect of a single case only, in particular Ps. 31.14[13]: Jer. 20.10, which does not necessarily also imply a statement of principle. But in most cases this is what it amounts to. It is characteristic of the whole approach that relatively little interest is devoted to the question. The only work that is rather more deeply concerned with it, W. Campe's *Das Verhältnis Jeremias zu den Psalmen* [The Relationship of Jeremiah to the Psalms] (1891), should therefore be briefly outlined. Campe thinks the majority of the parallels adduced by Hitzig should be rejected as merely coincidences in meaning due to the similarity of the situation and ideas; and on p. 11 he goes so far as to maintain that one might just as well, if not better, attribute the composition of these psalms to Isaiah or some other prophet. The only correspondences he will admit as true parallels are Ps. 6.2[1](38.2[1])//Jer. 10.24; Ps. 31.14a[13a]//Jer. 20.10a; Ps. 35.6a//Jer. 23.12a; Ps. 70.3[2]//Jer. 17.18; Ps. 79.6f.//Jer. 10.25 and Ps. 135.7//Jer. 10.13; in all of these he considers the priority to lie with Jeremiah. He does in the end admit, however,

> that in a number of passages Jeremiah's diction has a character similar to that of the Psalms ... And the elegiac tone of his diction, which shows particular affinities with the so-called psalms of lament, has its basis in the deep seriousness and dark melancholy of a man dismally afflicted by strokes of fate (p. 36).

The work suffers from the fault that in all cases it only sees points of contact between individual passages. Where Campe stops, the problem really begins.

Since this view pays insufficient regard to the unmistakably psalmic character of many a passage in Jeremiah, it has never been generally deemed satisfactory. B. Stade was the first to perceive correctly the attendant difficulty here and to seek to remove it, with his customary forcefulness, by excluding a series of such songs (10.23-25; 11.15–12.6; 14.7-10; 15.10-12, 15-19; 17; 20.7-18) as later additions; cf. *ZAW* 6 (1886), p. 153; *Geschichte des Volkes Israel*, I (1887), p. 646 (2nd edn; 1st edn p. 676); *Biblische Theologie des AT*, I (1905), p. 252, where he is again inclined to regard 11.18-23 and 12.5f. as authentic. His bold approach found little | [4] acceptance and few followers. Fr. Schwally disputed the authenticity of 15.10-18 (*ZAW* 10 [1890], p. 237) and A. Dillmann (*Hiob* [4th edn, 1891], p. xxxiii) that of 20.14-18. However, B. Duhm, *Das Buch Jeremiah* (1901), claimed that of all these songs only 10.23-25 and 12.1-6 did not derive from Jeremiah; he stood by the authenticity of the rest, rightly recognizing their prophetic character, and was content to delete only individual verses that were strongly reminiscent of the Psalms. In this he was supported by O. Kieser (*ThStKr* 78 [1905], pp. 507f.). Like Duhm, Cornill and Giesebrecht made do with few deletions, even fewer in fact; so, too, J.W. Rothstein in Kautzsch's *Heiliger Schrift des AT*, I (3rd edn, 1910). Stade's radical position found only two new representatives. According to Nath. Schmidt (*Encyclopaedia Biblica*, II [1901], pp. 2388f.)[4] the copyists and editors of the book of Jeremiah inserted a number of poetic passages and psalm fragments: 4.19-21; 8.18-23; 9.22f.; 10.19-21, 23-25; 11.15-17; 12.1-6, 7-13; 13.15-17; 14.2-6, 7-9, 19-21, 22; 15.5-9, 10, 11-14, 15-18, 19-21; 16.19f.; 17.1-4, 5-8, 9-11, 12f., 14-18; 20.7-13, 14-18. Similarly, G. Hölscher (*Die Profeten* [1914], pp. 396-99)—though with certain reservations—excludes as psalm-like additions: 10.23-25; 11.18-20; 12.1-6; 14.19-22; 15.10-12, 15-21; 16.19f.; 17.12f., 14-18; 18.18-23; 20.7-13, 14-18.

A quite different complexion was put on the question by the research on literary types (*Gattungsforschung*) introduced into Old Testament studies by H. Gunkel.[5] It established on one hand, by revealing the history of the spiritual Psalms that have come down to us, the greater antiquity of the poetry of the Psalms, and on the other hand it provided the first possibility of methodically comparing the psalm-like songs of Jeremiah with the Psalms. Gunkel reached the following conclusion: Jeremiah composed within the form of the psalms of lament but did not invent the psalms of lament type. Cf. his 'Israelitische Literatur', in *Kultur der Gegenwart*, Part I, Section VII (1906), pp. 87, 89; *RGG*, IV, col. 1942; *Reden und Aufsätze* (1913), p. 95; and in the introduction to H. Schmidt's *Die Großen Propheten* (1915), pp. lxiiif., lxxii. The same view was earlier held, independently of Gunkel, by W. Erbt, *Jeremia und seine Zeit* (1902), pp. 167-89, and a similar conclusion was subsequently reached by E. Balla, *Das Ich der Psalmen* [The 'I' of the Psalms] (1912), pp. 47-49, 51-56; | [5] H. Gressmann, *Die Schriften des AT in Auswahl* [The OT Scriptures—a selection] II/1 (1910), p. 327; M. Haller, *RGG*, III, col. 306; S. Mowinckel, *Zur Komposition des Buches Jeremia* (1914),

p. 60; H. Schmidt, *RGG*, II, col. 1155; *idem, Die religiöse Lyrik im AT* (1912), pp. 38-40, *Die großen Propheten* (1915); E. Sellin, *Einleitung in das AT* [OT Introduction] (1910), p. 110, (2nd edn, 1914, pp. 123f.); *idem, Zur Einleitung in das AT* (1912), pp. 63f., 84; W. Staerk, *Die Schriften des AT in Auswahl* III/1 (1910), pp. 152f.[6] The present investigation maintains the same position and aims to deal thoroughly and exhaustively with what could only be touched upon in the works just listed.

## Chapter 2

## THE INDIVIDUAL SONGS OF LAMENT TYPE[1]

About one third of all the songs of the Psalter belong to this type, namely Pss. 3; 4; 5; 6; 7; 11; 13; 16; 17; 22; 25; 26; 27;[2] 28; 31;[3] 35; 38; 39; 40.12-18[11-17]; 42/43; 51; 54; 55; 56; 57; 59; 61; 62; 63; 64; 69; 71; 77; 86; 88; 102.1-12, 24-29; 109; 119; 120; 123; 130; 140; 141; 142; 143; 144; also Lamentations 3. A number of songs from the book of Job, especially 10.1-22, are of a similar type. As particularly clear examples one might single out Pss. 3; 5; 6; 13; 22; 26; 28; 51; 54; 86; 140. For proof that in all these songs the subject is an individual person and not a majority group, the people or the community, we simply refer once and for all to Balla's work.

The 'communal' songs of lament have a similar structure and for the most part the same motifs and expressions; in these the majority laments over a calamity that has befallen the whole country. To these belong Pss. 9.18-21[17-20];[4] 10; 12; 44; 60.3-7, 11-14[1-5, 9-12]; 74; 79; 80; 83; 85.5-8[4-7]; 89.39-52[38-51]; 94; Lamentations 5. To complete the picture, we should take account | [7] of the thanksgiving songs, which already look back on the salvation implored in the songs of lament. Not only do they bear a strong resemblance to the songs of lament in their whole linguistic expression, but occasionally they quote part, or the whole, of the song of lament that was delivered at the time of distress; cf. Pss. 9.2-5, 14-17[1-4, 13-16]; 18; 30; 34; 40.1-11; 41; 66; 92; 116; 138; Isa. 38.10-20; Jon. 2.2-10; Sir. 51.1-12. Various ideas and motifs of the song of lament have occasionally penetrated into other literary types also, into hymns and didactic poems, so that here and there these will also need to be cited.

All songs of lament contain essentially the same subject-matter. The main components are as follows. As an introduction there is the 'invocation' of the deity. The main part, the 'corpus', contains the 'lament' and the 'petition', which is often accompanied by special motifs. The 'assurance of being heard', the 'vow', and often the hymnic 'thanksgiving' form the conclusion. There is, however, some degree of freedom in the sequence of the components. We shall now go through each of these parts in turn and consider them from the point of view of form and content.

## 1. *The Invocation*

The song of lament, like every prayer, begins with the invocation, the designation by name, of the deity to whom it is addressed. We thus invariably find in the first line of the song—the superscriptions which were added later do not count, of course—and often as the very first word, the name of God, Yahweh, Elohim or Adonai. Frequently the 'corpus', the lament or the petition, begins straightaway with the invocation:

> Yahweh, how many are my foes! (3.2[1])

> My God, my God, why hast thou forsaken me? (22.2[1])

Similarly, 6.2[1]; 7.2[1]; 10.1; 12.2[1]; 31.2[1]; 35.1; 38.2[1]; 42.2[1]; 56.2[1]; 59.2[1]; 70.2[1]; 71.1; 141.2[1]. The invocation can, however, be expanded and take the form of a special petition in which Yahweh is enjoined to be attentive and to hear the prayer.

> Give ear to my words, Yahweh;
> > give heed to my groaning (5.2[1]).

> To thee, Yahweh, I lift up my soul (25.1; cf. 86.4).

Similarly, 4.2[1]; 17.1; 27.7; 28.1f.; 55.2[1]; 61.2[1]; 77.1; 88.2f.[1f.]; 102.2[1]; 130.1f.; 141.1; 142.2f.[1f.]; 143.1. In accordance with the prayer style, Yahweh is usually directly addressed and is only rarely spoken of in the third person (77.2[1]; 142.2[1]). | [8]

This invocation then proceeds easily into the actual petition (64.2, 3[1, 2]; 86.1, 2; 102.2, 3[1, 2]) or is blended with it (54.3f.[1f.]; 57.2f. [1f.]). Elsewhere the lament follows first and the petition only after that (55.1-3, 4-9, 10ff.; cf. 88; 102; 142). Very exceptionally, the invocation does not come until near the end of the song (39.13[12], where the opening is also unusual).

## 2. *The Lament*

Here the psalmist describes his plight, in moving and sometimes quite passionate words. We hear much about weeping and sighing, anxiety and inner torment, sorrowful days and sleepless nights, sickness and persecution. Laments about physical and mental pain, mockery and harrassment, the calamity of war and the threat of floods intermingle confusedly, so that it is often not at all easy to tell what kind of calamity is involved in a particular case.

Not very frequent, but all the more valuable for that, are those passages which speak unambiguously of sickness.

> I am poured out like water,
>     and all my bones are out of joint;
> my heart is like wax,
>     it is melted within my breast;
> my throat[5] is dried up like a potsherd,
>     and my tongue cleaves to my gums (22.15f.).

His knees are weak from fasting, he has lost weight and become a shadow (109.23f.), his bones hang loosely under his skin (102.6[5]; Job 19.20)[6] and are easy to count (22.18[17]). Not one part of his body remains whole (38.4[3]), his skin is black and peeling off (Job 30.30), his wounds stink and fester (38.6[5]).

> For my days pass away like[7] smoke,
>     and my bones burn like a furnace (102.4[3]).

In the 'midst of his days', i.e. in his very prime, he thinks he must die (102.12, 24f.[11, 23f.]; Isa. 38.10; cf. Job 7.6). He feels in the grip of death, at the mercy of its horrors, standing right at the gates of the underworld (9.14[13]; 88.4-7[3-6]). | [9]

Much more often than sickness, however, mockery, persecution and harrassment are spoken of, frequently—oddly enough—in close connection with sickness:

> For they persecute him[8] whom thou hast smitten,
>     and increase[8] the pain of those whom thou hast wounded
>         (69.27).

The same picture emerges from 22.15-19[14-18]; 31.10-14[9-13]; 38.11-13[10-12]; 102.4-12[3-11]; 109.22-25. We should expect a sick man to be looked after and treated caringly; here he is persecuted and tormented all the more.[9] To understand this, we must extend our enquiry a little further.

It was a fundamental premise of Israelite religion that Yahweh treated all individuals according to their own deserts.[10] And everyday experience seemed to confirm this longing of the heart. Those who persevered in working and saving did well; those who neglected their work and led a dissolute life would one day be seen destitute. Such observations were generalized and the view became more and more firmly held that Yahweh blessed the pious and upright person with all earthly happiness—with health, a long life, many descendants, great possessions in cattle and land and rich harvests—but punished the godless and sinful person with all kinds of calamity—with sickness, unhappiness in the family, cattle diseases and poor harvests, or even with death. It was thus thought possible to draw conclusions about the conduct and character of particular people from their outward fate: prosperity proved piety, sickness and other plights betrayed the sinner.

But such a perspective as this, which is not in fact a specifically Israelite phenomenon at all but occurs everywhere at a certain cultural level, even though for many it became the cornerstone of their religion, did not remain undisputed. From approximately the end of the period of the monarchy onwards, the more intellectual circles in Israel began to peel away from the simple culture and religion inherited from of old[11] and, under the influence of foreign trends, to exchange it for shallow contempt and scepticism. Even just the picture of an inexorably recompensing God, and its consequence, the requirement of a strictly moral life-style, may have been uncomfortable to many. In addition, it was not difficult to refer to cases that clearly contradicted the rule. | [10] Thus to some degree two parties formed among the people. On the one hand the supporters of the doctrine of retribution, the 'pious', on the other their critics, the 'godless'. Many of our present songs of lament, and also the Job poem, grew out of such a situation.

Many a passage in the Psalms speaks of the ungodly. Usually, as is the way of simple narrative and graphic art, they are characterized by presenting their thoughts and speeches. They are unconcerned about Yahweh's punishing hand; for they think: 'The Lord does not see' (94.7). 'How can God know?' (73.11). 'Who will hear us?' (59.8[7]). 'Who can see us?' (64.6[5]). And even if he should see, 'he will not call to account' (10.4, 13), 'he will forget' (10.11)! They dispute that they have ever received good from him, and even say 'There is no God' (10.4; cf. 14.1). They act as if they could never be moved (10.5f.). In sum, the judgment on them is: they do not look to God (54.5[3]; 86.14) and 'revile' him (10.3, 13; 74.10, 18). Less frequently, their doings are directly described (10.3, 7-10; 13.3; 28.3).

Over against them stand the 'quiet in the land' (35.20), who have 'committed their cause to the Lord' (22.9[8]; 37.5; Prov. 16.3; cf. 22.11[10]; 55.23[22]). It will be best to think of them as a kind of small, pietistic conventicle, who separate themselves from the rest of the population but hold together all the more for that, sharing their joys and sorrows. Their own names for themselves are the 'righteous' (32.11; 33.1; 34.16[15]; 37.17, 29, 39, etc.), the 'upright in heart' (7.11[10]; 32.11; 37.14; 64.11[10]; 94.15), the 'saints' (31.24[23]; 37.28, etc.), while no names can be rude enough for their enemies— evil-doers, wicked, impious, etc.

As long as things go well for the pious, it is easy for them to withstand the attacks of their opponents. But then one of them falls sick. The others have been longing for this to happen. The news spreads round the neighbourhood like wildfire. And then they come, surround his camp, and grinning (40.15), they openly express their delight at his misfortune (35.15).

> He has committed[12] his cause to[13] the Lord,
> > let him rescue him, if he delights in him (22.9[8]).

But Yahweh does *not* rescue him, and they mock on:

> Where is your God? (42.4, 11[3, 10]; cf. 79.10)

Instead of them comforting him and cheering him up, he has to hear them whispering:

> |[11] When will he die, and his name perish?
> > He will not rise again from where he lies! (41.6, 9[5, 8])

And with that the gesticulating arms, the screaming voices, the grotesque, mocking faces!

> All who see me mock at me,
> > they make mouths at me, they wag their heads (22.8; cf. 35.19;
> > 109.25; Job 39.9-11).

In the gate, too, where people sit idly together, and in the wine house, they laugh about him (69.13[12]). To be the object of general laughter like this, to be gossiped about, is a horrific thing to the oriental, almost harder to bear than the sickness itself. Nobody takes his part.

> I look to the right and watch,
> > but there is none who takes notice of me;

> no refuge remains to me,
>> no-one cares for me (142.5[4]).

Even those who are closest to him now run from him (38.12[11]; 88.9, 19[8, 18]).

> Even my bosom friend in whom I trusted,
>> who ate of my bread, has lifted his heel against me (41.10[9]).
> 'It is not an enemy who taunts me—
>> then I could bear it;
> it is not an adversary who deals insolently with me—
>> then I could hide from him.
> But it is you, my equal,
>> my companion, my familiar friend.
> We used to hold sweet converse together
>> within God's house' (55.13-15[12-14]; cf. 31.12-14[11-13]; Job
>> 6.15; 16.20; 19.13-20).

His own brothers turn their backs on him (69.9[8]), and father and mother forsake him (27.10).

We should not simply count this as heartlessness and betrayal on their part. They too stand under the sway of the theory of retribution and are acting in accordance with it in good faith. God's arrows have hit the sick man (38.3[2]; Job 6.4), God's hand has struck him (69.27[26]; Job 19.21). And so those who were hitherto his friends and comrades have to have their doubts about him: obviously he must have sinned in secret, perhaps he has been a terrible hypocrite. And was not the whole party of the pious now put in a bad light and exposed? God himself has now marked him out and thus he is to be avoided. 'A deadly thing has fastened upon him' (41.9[8])—how easy it would be | [12] to catch it from him! He has become 'a thing of horror' (88.9[8]);[14] if he looks around: 'terror on every side' (31.14[13])!

Good friends will also try to bring him to a confession of his sins, as Job's friends do, wanting to get to the root of the matter (Job 19.28).[15] Or all kinds of things are suspected, so that soon the most horrific stories circulate about him. 'Aha, Aha! our eyes have seen it!' (35.20f.) Such are the insults and lies about which the psalmist so often bitterly complains (4.3[2]; 12.3, 5[2, 4]; 31.19, 21[18, 20]; 35.20; 38.21[20]; 55.4[3]; 59.13[12]; 62.5[4]; 140.4[3]), the tongues that are sharp as swords and pointed as arrows (57.5[4]; 64.4f.[3f.]; 120.2-4; 140.4[3]), the false witnesses that appear against him (27.12; 35.11).

And so finally the border between friend and foe almost disappears. Everyone has become his enemy, and he stands quite alone against the 'many' (3.3[2]; 4.7[6]; 31.14[13]; 55.19[18]; 56.3[2]; 119.157; cf. 3.2[1]; 25.19; 38.20[19]; 69.5[4]).

They are after his life, we are frequently told, (35.4; 38.13[12]; 40.15[14]; 54.5[4]; 70.3[2]; 86.14), either secretly lying in wait for him and plotting all kinds of things against him (5.11[10]; 10.2; 21.12[11]; 35.4, 20; 41.8[7]; 140.3, 5[2, 4]); or openly attacking him (17.9-11; 22.17[16]; 54.5[3]; 86.14; Job 16.9-14), inciting one another: 'Pursue and seize him!' (71.11; cf. 74.8;[16] 83.5[4]). If it were not for Yahweh's last-minute intervention they would be able to triumph: 'We have prevailed over him!' (13.4; 35.25). On the frequent occasions when in the same context a single individual is suddenly spoken of (7.2f.[1f.]; 17.12; 55.21f.[20f.]; 109.6), the person in question will be the ring-leader, assuming the text is in order.

For the most part, however, these attacks are spoken of only in images, using expressions taken from the hunt, some of which also reappear in proverbial wisdom. The psalmist complains that in his 'haunt' (140.6[5]; 142.4[3]) they have dug traps for him (בור, שוחה, שחת, 7.16[15]; 9.16[15]; 35.7) as one would for wild animals; that they lay snares for him, set traps and spread nets (מוקש, פח, רשת, 9.16[15]; 25.15; 31.5; 35.7; 38.13[12]; 57.7[6]; 64.6[5]; 91.3; 119.110; 140.6[5]; 141.9f.; 142.4[3]), as is the custom in hunting birds. He compares his enemies to a pack of baying dogs worrying a noble wild animal to death (22.17, 21[16, 20]), or with the semi-wild stray dogs that make the city streets unsafe in the evenings (59.7f., 15f.[6f., 14f.]). Also favoured is the comparison with wild bulls (22.13, 22[12, 21]) or with lions (7.3[2]; 10.9; 17.12; 22.14, 22[13, 21]).

| [13] In other passages again it seems to be a question of war.

> I am not afraid of ten thousands of people
> > who have set themselves against me round about
> > > (3.7[6]; cf. 27.3; 35.1-3; 56.2).

But the fact that these enemies are in the same breath described in the usual way as ungodly men (35.4, 11ff.) leads us to suspect that here too—with the possible exception of 144.1-11, where it seems that a prince does actually speak—we are presented with mere metaphors, which may, however go back to earlier war songs. That such passages should not be understood literally is shown, for example, by 11.2:

> For lo, the wicked bend their bow,
> > they have their arrow to the string,
> > to shoot in the dark at the upright in heart.

The bows here are clearly nothing other than the malicious tongues that have been mentioned, and the arrows nothing but their lies and slanderous insults. Such imagery helps, precisely by means of its inherent exaggeration, to increase the impression of plight and to make the petition appear so much the more urgent. Occasionally the psalmist even speaks of 'a people' that is persecuting him (43.1),[17] and sees 'nations' storming against him (9.16, 18[15, 17]; 56.8[7]; 59.6, 9[5, 8]).[18]

The use of another image strikes us as more strange. For often the psalmist complains of floods that threaten to swallow him up, of a pit, of dung and mire in which he is in danger of sinking. The same expressions recur in the petition and in the recital of the thanksgiving song. They are not to be taken literally—as did Hitzig, for example, who connected them with particular episodes in Jeremiah's life—but metaphorically.[19] They are terms, taken from ancient mythological concepts, for the underworld—which is occasionally explicitly mentioned—and its parts; ultimately it concerns the journey to the underworld of a hero or a god.[20] By his exaggeration, which we have been able to observe at many points, the psalmist, lying on his sickbed, and in some cases, perhaps, truly | [14] in mortal danger, claims to be near the underworld, even to have already descended into it and to be at the mercy of all its horrors (9.14[13]; 16.10; 18.5f., 17[4f., 16]; 30.4[3]; 40.3[2]; 42.8[7]; 49.16[15]; 69.2f., 15f.[1f., 14f.]; 71.20; 86.13; 88.4f., 7[3f., 6] 94.17; 107.18, 20; 116.3; 124.4f.; 130.1; Isa. 38.10f.; Jon. 2.4, 6f.[3, 5f.]; Job 33.28; Lam. 3.53f.; Sir. 51.2, 6, 9).

If one wants to reach a correct understanding of the songs one has to be clear as to which of all these complaints may be taken literally and which are metaphors or decorative exaggerations. We should not expect a simple presentation of the underlying facts. In response to the cruel glee of his opponents, the sick man brings all his passion to bear on the battle, which with his oriental temperament he does not find difficult anyway. Perhaps the 'attacks' and 'attempts on his life' never even went beyond battles of words, open contempt and surreptitious gossip. We must ascribe this to the unfortunate man's state of excitement and we shall not need to assume intentional exaggeration and distortion at all.

The psalmist draws a really pitiful picture of himself:

But I am a worm and no man;
    scorned by men, and despised by the people (22.7[6]).

He likes to call himself 'poor' (עני 10.2, 9; 22.25[24]; 25.16; 34.7[6];
35.10; 37.14; 40.18[17]; 69.30[29]; 74.21; 86.1; 88.16[15]; 109.16, 22)
and 'needy'[21] (אביון 9.19[18]; 35.10; 37.14; 40.18[17]; 74.21; 82.4;
86.1; 107.41; 109.16, 22, 31; 113.7), 'weak' (9.10[9]; 10.18), 'lonely'
(25.16), and he tenderly speaks of his soul as his 'only one'
(22.21[20]; 35.17), his 'afflicted' (22.22[21]) one.[22] And it is easy for
thoughts about the transitoriness of man in general to be added to
the complaints about the wasting-away of his own life (39.5-7, 12[4-
6, 11]; 49.6-15[5-14]; 62.10[9]; 90.3-10; 144.3f.; Job 7.1-10; 14.1-
12).

Perhaps even more than by sickness, persecution and forsakenness,
he is tormented by spiritual pain. Has his trust in God been in vain?
Or has he really—perhaps unknowingly—been guilty of such serious
sin? Either alternative would be as terrible for him as the other. In
any case he now sees his expectations disappointed and his
confidence shattered. It is this feeling that is described by the verbs
בוש, חפר, כלם (niph.), 'to let down',| [15] one might almost say, rather
more bluntly, 'to be made a fool of'.[23] The psalmist thus complains
that Yahweh has already let him down (44.10[9]) and in him the
whole party of the pious also (69.7[6]), or he asks that He might not
put him to shame (25.2, 20; 31.2[1]; 71.1; 119.6, 31, 46, 80, 116), so
that the enemy might not triumph (25.2; 94.3).

In this state of despair he does not even spare Yahweh in his
reproaches.

    For it is for thy sake that I have borne reproach.
        that shame has covered my face (69.8[7]; cf. 44.23[22];
            69.10[9]; 119.139).

He finds Yahweh's behaviour all the more incomprehensible because
of this. Often a painful 'why?' thus breaks from him—always למה,
never מדוע. 'Why hast thou forsaken me?' (22.2[1]). Why hast thou
forgotten me?' (42.10[9]; 44.25[24]). 'Why hast thou cast me off?'
(43.2; 74.1; 88.15[14]). 'Why dost thou stand afar off?' (10.1; 22.2[1]).
'Why sleepest thou?' (44.24[23]). Cf. further 74.11; 79.10; 80.12;
115.2.—And along with this the other question, 'how long?'

    How long, O Lord? Wilt thou forget me for ever?
    How long wilt thou hide thy face from me?

> How long must I bear pain in my heart,
> > Sorrow in my soul, day and night? [24] (13.2f.[1f.]).

Such a quotation is introduced by מתי (42.3[2]), עד־מתי (6.4[3]; 74.10; 80.5[4]; 90.13; 94.3), עד־מה (4.3[2]; 79.5; 89.47[46]), עד־אנה (13.2f.[1f.]). Other questions of a similar sort also crop up (cf. 77.8-10[7-9]). It is always the same thoughts that keep recurring: that Yahweh has forgotten him, forsaken him, is no longer concerned about him and stands far off. Is it a coincidence that we have already met these same thoughts in the mouths of the wicked?[25] In the moments of his greatest forsakenness and despair the unfortunate man's mind is filled with what to the wicked is a basic fact of life, their world-view, but to him is a harrowing question, a vexing doubt. For him, however, it is not the end of the matter.

The most important ideas of the lament have now been mentioned. It is, of course, an overall picture, and many of the individual songs only display sections of it. In particular, in a whole series of songs there is no allusion at all to sickness (4; 5; 7; 11; 17; 27; 52; 54; 55; 57; 59; 62-64; 120; 123; 130; 140-142; 144). Only mockery and hostility | [16] are spoken of here. The basic cause may still be sickness, however, in the manner we have described; but we may also consider whether perhaps we have a further development of the literary type here, with, over a period of time, the reasons for songs of lament becoming more generalized, and in particular other social and religious antagonisms entering in.[26] Indeed, some Psalms (25; 119), seem not to have arisen from any particular distress situation at all but seem rather to be only concerned with the general theme of the righteous and the wicked. Thus the song of lament becomes a general prayer.

The outward extent of the lament varies a great deal in the songs. Sometimes it is quite short, just a brief justification of the request (6.3f.[2f.]) or can be inferred only from the petition (26.9). When elaborated, however, it can extend over a series of verses (22.7-9, 13-19[6-8, 12-18]), and in some circumstances even comprise the major part of the whole song (10; 38; Lam. 5). One song (88) consists entirely of invocation and lament, thus ending, like most of the songs of lament in the book of Job, without so much as the faintest expression of hope.

### 3. *The Petition*

After the lament, the petition is the most important part of the song. It is often introduced by a request for Yahweh's intervention, similar to what we found in the invocation: 'Arise' (3.8[7]; 7.7[6]; 10.12; 17.13; 35.2; 44.27[26]; 74.22), 'awake' (7.7[6]; 35.23; 44.24[23]; 59.5f. [4f.]), 'make haste' (22.20[19]; 38.23[22]; 40.14[13]; 70.2[1]; 71.12; 141.1), 'look down from heaven and see' (80.15[14]), 'consider my affliction and my trouble' (25.18; cf. 13.4[3]; 59.5[4]), 'turn to me' (25.16), 'be gracious to me' (4.2[1]; 6.3[2]; 9.14[13]; 25.16; 26.11; 27.7; 31.10[9]), 'answer me' (4.2[1]; 7.10[9];[27] 13.4[3]; 27.7), 'hear my supplication' (28.2)!

If the petition is a negative one, it corresponds to the relevant expressions of the lament. 'Forsake me not' (27.9; 38.22[21]; 71.9, 18; 119.8), 'do not abandon me' (44.24[23]), 'forget not' (10.12), 'be not silent' (28.1; 35.22; 39.13[12]; 83.2[1]; 109.1), 'be not far from me' (22.12, 20[11, 19]; 35.22; 38.22[21]; 71.12)!

Seldom is there a request for healing, even in cases where there is no doubt that sickness is the concern.

Heal me, for my bones are troubled (6.3[2]; cf. 41.5[4]).

| [17] Rather, the petition is really more concerned with forgiveness of sins; for the view is that along with the sin, its consequence, sickness, will also be removed.

According to thy abundant mercy blot out my transgressions
Wash me thoroughly from my iniquity
    and cleanse me from my sin! (51.3f.[1f.])
Purge me with hyssop, and I shall be clean (51.9[7]).

More frequently the concern is for deliverance from the external affliction.

Keep me as the apple of thy eye;
    hide me in the shadow of thy wings (17.8; cf. 5.9[8]; 16.1).
Save me from all my pursuers (7.2[1]; cf. 25.20).
Sweep me not away with sinners,
    nor my life with bloodthirsty men (26.9; cf. 28.3).

For a sudden death in the prime of life would be regarded as punishment for some serious sin (37.2).

Frequently, however, especially in those songs that no longer emanate from a particular distress situation, the petition is kept much more general and spiritualized, and desirous of moral instruction and preservation from evil.

> Make me to know thy ways, O Lord;
>> teach me thy paths.
> Lead me in thy truth and teach me,
>> for thou art the God of my salvation (25.4f.).

Similarly, 27.11; 51.12f.[10f.]; 86.11; 119.33-40; 143.10.

Just as certain metaphorical phrases constantly occur in the lament, so here do a number of expressions which in fact derive from a quite different sphere of life and which therefore require special elucidation. The psalmist likes to compare himself with someone involved in a legal dispute (ריב, 35.23), who turns to the judge—in this case, Yahweh—for help. The term for this is זעק or צעק (22.6[5]; 34.18[17]; 77.2[1]; 88.2[1]; 107.6, 28; 142.2, 6[1, 5], and often in Job, צעקה, 9.13), which contains both lament and petition. It is the cry of complaint and the cry for help of someone who has suffered injustice and violence at the hands of a more powerful person; cf. Gen. 4.10, Exod. 2.23; 3.7; Deut. 22.24, 27; 2 Sam. 19.29; 1 Kgs 20.39; 2 Kgs 4.1; 6.26; 8.3, 5; Hab. 1.2; Job 19.7; 31.38; Esth. 4.1. The piel of שוע is also used in the same sense (18.7[6]; 22.25[24]; 28.2; 30.3[2]; 31.23[22]; 88.14[13]; 119.147; שׁוְעָה 18.7[6]; 34.16[15]; 39.13[12]; 40.2[1]; 102.2; 145.19; cf. Exod. 2.23; Job 19.7). We have to imagine oriental legal conditions, not of course those of highly developed constitutional states such as Babylon and Assyria, but those with a simpler culture. There is always the poor man who is suffering injustice and who therefore goes to the judge or the king | [18] (2 Sam. 14.4ff.; 15.2ff.; 2 Kgs 6.26ff.; 8.3ff.; Lk. 18.2ff.). The reverse case, whereby a rich man is wronged, will occur rarely enough, and should it occur, the latter is more likely to know how to obtain his rights. Only the poor man is completely dependent on the mercy of the judge, and when he begs, 'Judge me!', the meaning is: 'Help me gain my rights'. The psalmist also makes such requests (7.9[8]; 26.1; 35.24; 43.1), taking for granted that he is in the right and innocent (7.9[8]; 26.1). דין also is used (54.1), in the same sense as שפט.

Yahweh is thought of as judge (cf. 1 Sam. 24.16; Prov. 22.23; 23.11), and not as the counsel who helps him present his case in court, even when the petition is 'plead my cause' (ריבה ריבי, 43.1; 119.154). But it can also be 'plead *thy* cause' (74.22); the thought then is that Yahweh is himself insulted by the words and deeds of the wicked and has his honour to protect.

In all these petitions the psalmist is not merely concerned with his own person, though this does of course come first. At the same time he thinks of his comrades, who are also affected by his misfortune. He asks, too, that they may not be put to shame on his account (69.7[6]), but be able cheerfully to hold their heads high and rejoice (5.12[11]; 35.27; 40.17[16]).

The request for his own salvation and vindication is matched on the other hand by his request for the punishment of his enemies.

> Requite them according to their work
> and according to the evil of their deeds!
>     (28.4; cf. 10.15; 140.9-12[8-11]; 143.12)

They, who now triumph over his fall, should be made to witness his happiness (23.5) and should see their own plans go awry. They should be put to shame (cf. 31.17f.; 35.4-6; 40.14f.; 70.2f.), and should themselves fall into the snares they have set up (5.11[10]; 35.8; 141.10); the underworld should swallow them alive (55.16[15]; cf. 63.10f.[9f.]). Sometimes this request is even elaborated into a terrible curse (69.23-29[22-28]; 109.6-20). Such sentiments come as an unpleasant surprise next to the many tender aspects that are particularly prevalent in these songs. But the fact is that both are at home in the breast of the psalmist, and the malicious glee of the wicked finds its counterpart here.

### 4. *Motifs*

Israelite prayer is childishly simple.[28] Like a child that wants to beg something of its father, seeking first to put him in an agreeable mood with flattery and tenderness, so does the human being act | [19] towards the deity. Half consciously, half unconsciously, all kinds of 'motifs' creep into the prayer, designed to lend emphasis to the petition and bring about a more favourable reception.

1. The petitioner thus likes to complain to Yahweh that he is having to suffer so much for his sake (69.8, 10[7, 9]; 119.139). In so doing he appeals to his *honour*, hoping at the same time to convince him that his own reputation is at stake. This idea is of course given more place and more justification in the communal song of lament (44.23[22]; 74.2-10, 18, 22f.; 79.9-12; 83.19[18]).

2. More important and more frequent than this honour motif is the *trust motif*. Here the psalmist clings to his God in the firm confidence

that he will not let him down. This trust is capable of many forms of expression. Often it says simply: 'In thee I trust' (13.6[5]; 25.2; 26.1; 28.7; 31.7, 15[6, 14]; 52.10[8]; 55.24[23]; 56.4f., 12[3f., 11]; 119.42; 143.8), 'in thee do I take refuge' (7.2[1]; 11.1; 16.1; 25.20; 31.2[1]; 71.1; 141.8; 144.2), 'my hope is in thee' (25.5, 21; 38.16[15]; 39.8[7]; 40.2[1]; 52.11[9]; 69.4[3]; 71.14; 119.43, 74, 81, 114, 147; 130.5). Yahweh is described as the object of this trust in the most varied expressions, as shield (3,4[3]; 7.11[10]; 18.3[2]), rock (18.3[2]; 28.1; 31.4[3]; 62.3, 7[2, 6]), refuge (18.3[2]; 27.1; 31.3f.[2f.]; 43.2), stronghold (9.10[9]; 18.3[2]; 62.3, 7[2, 6]). He calls him 'God of my salvation' (25.5; 27.9) or just 'my God' (7.2[1]; 25.2; 31.15[14]), reminds him of his mercy and goodness (6.5[4]; 31.17[16]; 51.3[1]; 109.21), builds upon his righteousness (5.5ff.[4ff.]; 7.10ff.[9ff.]; 11.5ff.[4ff.]), his long-suffering (86.5, 15) and his willingness to forgive (86.5; 130.4). He remembers how Yahweh has always shown him goodness thus far (22.10f.[9f.]; 25.6; 71.6, 17f.; 139.13ff.); if it had not been for him he would not be there at all (94.17f.). He is comforted too by the thought of Yahweh's deeds in past ages (44.2, 4[1, 3]; 143.5), and his words quite automatically obtain a hymnic sound:

> Yet thou art throned as the holy one,
>     Israel's praise.[29]
> In thee our fathers trusted;
>     they trusted, and thou didst deliver them.
> To thee they cried, and were saved;
>     in thee they trusted, and were not disappointed (22.4-6[3-5]).

Similarly, 11.4; 31.20f.[19f.]; 86.8-10; 102.26-28[25-27]—a shattering contrast to his own plight.

It is with thoughts such as these that the trust-motif is woven into the petition. It is the basis on which the latter rests. Without this trust he would not even dare to cherish a hope and make a petition. | [20] Sometimes it comes right at the beginning of the song (7.2[1]; 31.2[1]) or forms the refrain (56.5, 11f.[4, 10f.]; 62.2f., 6f.[1f., 5f.]), a number of times taking the form—as in the individual hymn (104.1; 146.1)—of the psalmist addressing his own soul, exhorting it to trust (42.6, 12[5, 11]; 43.5; cf. 27.14; 55.23[22]).

Since this motif is in essence particularly close to the heart of the pious, it could easily separate itself from the song of lament, the ground on which it grew, and become independent of it. The simple, childlike trust that does not grasp after things, that is in want for nothing, since it already has everything, now finds expression—often with no special plight or particular petition as its cause. This is how the psalms of trust that are so dear to us came into being (16; 23; 27.1-6; 62; 121)—some of the most beautiful and intimate songs of the whole Psalter.

3. The *repentance motif*. Since, according to the theory of retribution, some guilt must lie at the root of his suffering, the sick man is moved to soul-searching and contemplation. In sleepless nights he searches through his past, pondering over where he might have been at fault. And what a lot he finds there that he would never otherwise have thought of! They now surface, all his sins from his early youth onwards—now he knows why he is suffering.

> For evils have encompassed me without number;
> > my iniquities have overtaken me (40.13[12]).
> My transgressions have prevailed over me (65.4[3]).

He has to confess his sin (38.19[18]; and if he tries to keep it quiet, he does not succeed anyway (32.3-5). And so he asks Yahweh to remember the sins of his youth no more (25.7) and to forgive him in spite of their number (25.11, 18).

> O God, thou knowest my folly;
> > the wrongs I have done are not hidden from thee (69.6[5]).
> Enter not into judgment with thy servant;
> > for no-one living is righteous before thee (143.2).
> If thou, O Lord, shouldst mark iniquities,
> > Lord, who could stand? (130.3).

By his open confession he wants to relieve his conscience and presumably hopes he will be able thereby to appease Yahweh's anger somewhat also.

4. However, this is not an invariable perspective. Almost as frequently we find the *innocence motif*. In this case, the psalmist knows of no sin and feels completely pure (7.9[8]; 17.1; 26.1, 11; 41.13[12]). Yahweh himself can find no fault in him (17.3-5; 26.2; cf. 66.18 in the | [21] thanksgiving song), though he tests him thoroughly right to his 'heart and reins' (7.10[9]; 11.4f.; 17.3; 26.2; 66.10; 69.9; 139.23) and knows him through and through (40.10[9]; 139.2, 4; 142.4[3]). He appeals to the fact that he has always avoided the company of evil men and has been mindful of Yahweh (18.21-25[20-24]; 26.3-5; 44.18-22[17-21] [communal]; 119.157-168; Job 23.10-12; 31) and has fulfilled his cultic duties (26.6-8); and to the fact that he

acted quite differently towards tnose who are now behaving so shabbily towards him, when they themselves were sick (35.12-14), whereas they now recompense him with ingratitude (38.21[20]; 109.5). This protestation of innocence can extend to the ritual oath (7.4-6[3-5]) or find expression in the washing of hands (26.6; 73.13[12]), a symbolic act (Mt. 27.24) which in former times was a cultic act, a purification rite (cf. Deut. 21.6). In such contexts the petition is frequently desirous not of mercy but of justice (7.9[8]; 26.1), but on the whole the ideas are not so sharply distinguished.

Taken alongside those expressions of a profound awareness of sin, such protestations of innocence may easily seem to us to be superficial and self-righteous, and indeed these psalms are often called simply 'self-righteousness psalms' [*Selbstgerechtigkeitspsalmen*]. This may be appropriate in one or two cases, but for the type *per se* it would surely be an unfair judgment. The awareness of sin may in many cases not simply be due to the objections of the conscience; it was possible for those bound by the doctrine of retribution to try in this way to account for, and rid themselves of, sickness or other misfortunes. There were great moral dangers inherent in this, as the book of Job clearly shows, and it will scarcely have been the worst people who resisted this temptation and refused to eat humble pie against their conscience. Psalm 32 perhaps shows how someone who has bravely defended himself or herself for a long time gives way after all in the end.[31] But others held out steadfastly and did not allow themselves to be swayed by all the talk and coaxing around them. To them it was a matter of conscience—a healthy and extremely necessary reaction against the theory of retribution whose constraints reduce everything to the same level.[32]

Moreover, one should not simply look for claims to absolute sinlessness in these protestations of innocence. Often it is only the gross sins that are in mind, while the possibility of smaller, especially | [22] unintentional, trangressions is not excluded (cf. 19.12). The psalmists feel their innocence especially in comparison with their persecutors, who openly exhibit so many more serious faults. So they will feel guilty before Yahweh, but before him alone (51.6[4])—for what person could stand before Yahweh! (130.3; 143.2)—but in relation to them, innocent (59.4f.[3f.], and tormented by them (25.3; 35.7, 19; 38.19; 69.4; 109.3; 119.78, 86, 161) 'without cause' (שקר, ריקם, חנם).

Now and then the psalmist points out to Yahweh what little benefit he would draw from the death of his devoted servant.

> What profit is there in my death,
>     if I go down to the Pit?
> Will the dust praise thee?
>     Will it tell of thy faithfulness? (30.10[9]).

The same idea recurs in 6.6[5]; 88.11-13[10-12]; 115.17; Isa. 38.18f.; Sir. 17.27f.; Bar. 2.17f. Down into the latest period the old view perseveres, that Yahweh's sphere of influence extends only to the earth and that he has no authority in the underworld. If Yahweh lets the psalmist die he will thereby lose his singer; the psalmist seeks in all simplicity to impress this upon Yahweh. In the song of lament (6; 30;[33] 88), this motif serves to move Yahweh to intervene; in the thanksgiving song (Isa. 38) its purpose is to explain the rescue that has occurred.

### 5. *The Assurance of Being Heard*

Some psalms close with the petition (38; 39; 44) or with the trust-motif (40b; 55). In others we find a quite abrupt transition from lament or petition to a quite different mood. Psalm 6 may serve as an example. This begins with a request (v. 2[1]), followed by petition and lament (vv. 3f.[2f.]), petition (v. 5[4]) with motif (v. 6[5]), lament (vv. 7f.[6f.]); and then suddenly we read:

> Depart from me, all you workers of evil;
>     for the Lord has heard the sound of my weeping.
> The Lord has heard my supplication;
>     the Lord has accepted[34] my prayer.
> All my enemies shall be ashamed and sorely troubled;[35]
>     they shall turn back, and be put to shame in a moment (6.9-
>         11[8-10]).

| [23] The same thing occurs in 3.5[4]; 4.4, 8f.[3, 7f.]; 10.16-18; 26.12; 28.6f.; 31.6b-9, 22[5b-8, 21]; 56.14[13]; 64.8f.[7f.]. In all these cases the rescue appears as a *fait accompli* in the perfect or imperf. cons.: Yahweh has heard my prayer, he *has* saved me. Elsewhere this confident mood is expressed in the imperfect.

> Thou wilt not give me up to Sheol,
>     or let thy godly one see the Pit (16.10f.).

17.15; 35.8-10; 60.14; 71.20f. read similarly. Since in the Hebrew the jussive and indicative of the imperfect are no longer distinguished in most cases, one can often be unsure whether an imperfect should be translated in jussive mood as a petition ('may he') or in indicative mood as a certainty ('he will'). In substance the difference is not very great anyway.

The perfect and the imperfect forms of the assurance are used in the same way. Common to both is the contrast to the mood of lament and petition. What then seemed far off and was earnestly desired is now becoming, or even has already become, reality. One could define this mood as an expression of the height of trust; having arrived at the climax of the prayer, the psalmist experiences in advance that for which he is so fervently imploring, as if it had already happened. This is felt to be a good note on which to conclude the song (4; 10; 26; 56). Less frequently the psalmist afterwards reverts to the lament, and usually only to soar up to that height a second time (31; 86).

We should perhaps see as a counterpart to the assurance of being heard the promissory oracle that appears in its place at various points (12.6[5]; cf. 60.5-11[6-9]; 91.14-16),[36] which also serves the same function as far as its content is concerned.

### 6. *Vow and Thanksgiving*

Whenever the psalmist can see that what he is praying for has already happened, he then adds what he intends to do in God's honour from now on, since God has rescued him from his plight. The vow is thus usually set towards the end of the song. | [24]

> I will praise thy mercy[37] in the great congregation;
>     my vow will I pay before those who fear him.
> The meek shall eat and be satisfied.
>     those who seek him shall praise Yahweh.
> May your hearts be refreshed for ever! (22.26f.[25f.]; cf. 54.8f.[6f.];
>     56.13[12]).

But for the most part sacrifices are no longer spoken of. The psalmist knows—doubtless a consequence of the rejection of the sacrificial cult by the prophets—that another gift will please Yahweh far more:

> O Lord, open thou my lips,
>     and my mouth shall show forth thy praise.

> For thou hast no delight in meal offerings;
> > were I[38] to give a whole offering, thou wouldst not be
> > pleased.
> God's meal-offering is a broken spirit;
> > a broken heart, Yahweh, thou wilt not despise
> > > (51.17-19[15-17]; cf. 69.31f.[30f.] and in the thanksgiving
> > > song 40.7-11[6-10]).

The song thus takes the place of the sacrifice. In the circle of his household and friends, or even before an assembled congregation, he wants to relate what Yahweh has done and extol his might and his goodness (7.18[17]; 13.6b; 22.23, 26[22, 25]; 26.12; 28.7; 31.8[7]; 35.18, 28; 42.6, 12[5, 11]; 43.4f.; 51.17[15]; 52.11[9]; 54.8[6]; 57.8-11[7-10]; 59.17[16]; 61.9[8]; 69.31-37[30-36]; 71.14-16, 22-24; 109.30f.; 119.171f., 175; 142.8[7]; 144.9f.). Often it is explicitly emphasized that this is to take place before a large assembly, before all the righteous (35.18; 52.11[9]; 109.30)—in one case, with the customary exaggeration, it even says 'among the nations' (57.10[9])—for, just as the sick man's sufferings affected all his comrades too, so also his salvation and vindication will now be joyfully celebrated by everyone.

> The righteous will surround me;
> > for thou wilt deal bountifully with me (142.8b[7b]; cf.
> > 5.12[11]; 22.27[26]; 35.27; 40.17[16]; 64.11; 69.33f.[32f.];
> > 140.14[13]).

He is then free from the humiliating suspicion, and the victory of the righteous is evident. A secondary purpose of the thanksgiving celebrations is to make an impression on the apostates and sinners (51.15[13]).

The thanksgiving song that is to be sung on this occasion follows on quite naturally from the vow.

> You who fear Yahweh, praise him!
> > all you sons of Jacob, honour him,
> > and tremble before him, all you sons of Israel!
> | [25] For he has not despised or abhorred
> > to answer[39] the poor man;
> and he has not hid his face from him,
> > but has heard his crying (22.24f.[23f.]; cf. 69.36f.[35f.]; 144.9f.).

A thanksgiving song such as this, with the usual structure— introduction, narrative and confession in hymnic tones,[40] or an equivalent hymn—may also follow on from the assurance of being heard (31.22-25[21-24]; 35.10; 57.8b-11[7b-10]), or follow straight on from the petition without any apparent connection (28.6-8). In his anticipation of the joy to come the psalmist's soul rises above and beyond the present distress.

## 7. *The Songs of Lament as a whole*

The songs of lament thus agree in subject matter and form at many points. On the other hand this type is extraordinarily developed; just from the large number of songs that are to be included within it, one can see how popular it must have been. It was cultivated for centuries, and, for all its dependence on the old forms of expression, it was always creating new ones. Hence the great variety within this literary type, far exceeding, for example, that in the thanksgiving psalms. It is not just that often one part or even several are missing, so that in fact only the lament and the petition should be regarded as the indispensable constituents of the song of lament. There is a great deal of freedom in the arrangement itself, and the picture is made even more colourful by the fact that the lament and the petition in particular occur at various times and places in the same song. The psalmist is especially partial to alternating between lament and petition two or three times, sometimes including the trust motif as well (22; 31; 35; 55; 59; 69; 79; 80). To our differently trained sense of style, a song like this necessarily creates an impression of great disorder: instead of a strict progression of ideas there is a restless to-ing and fro-ing of ideas. But it would be quite wrong to try to introduce some order by always placing similar ideas together.[41] The apparent disorder corresponds to the psalmist's excited state of mind. It is an attempt, albeit a schematized one, to express the ups and downs of his mood, his wavering between dark hopelessness and firm confidence, timorous petition and victorious assurance.

| [26] Precisely because of this variegation in the arrangement of the songs it is difficult for the modern reader to recognize that they belong to a particular literary type. But the points of agreement do predominate despite all the freedom in details. In content and design they are all so similar to one another that, read one after the other, they appear thoroughly monotonous. This similarity cannot be due simply to coincidence, nor is it explicable on the grounds that roughly the same situation underlies each case. The agreement in the

use of particular, almost formalized expressions and stereotyped metaphors—would be even less likely a consequence of coincidence than the correspondence in the whole layout. This is only understandable if not simply the content of such songs was to some extent established by custom and tradition but also there was a stock of firmly established turns of phrase and images from which each new singer, consciously or unconsciously, would draw. And this was greatly facilitated when the situation in each case and the psalmist's own experience pointed in the same direction anyway.

Now in our songs a few scattered expressions are to be found, such as the 'washing of hands in innocence' (26.6; 73.13) and the petition for absolution with hyssop (51.9[7]), which, though at this stage they are only metaphors, nevertheless doubtless derive from actual cultic customs, cultic washing (cf. Deut. 21.6) and the purging of the penitent by the priest with a hyssop (cf. Lev. 14.4ff., 51). This sheds light on the original background of our songs: the sick man came into the sanctuary, where he performed his song, in which he begged for forgiveness of his sin and healing of his sickness. The answer of the priest, who mediated the decision of the oracle—oracles still occur occasionally in our songs (p. 36)—was linked with all kinds of ceremonies.

The purely spiritual songs of lament that we have in the Psalter must therefore have been preceded by *cultic* songs of lament;[48] in other psalm types, especially in the thanksgiving songs, they are still present in our texts (cf. Pss. 66.13ff.; 107.21f.; 116.13f., 17f.). We now understand better why they all resemble one another so much. Cultic language is less free and is always inclined to the formation of established forms—a consequence of the originally magical significance of their wording. And with the constant repetition of the same forms a firm style was bound to develop. Here, as in the very similar case of the thanksgiving songs, one may perhaps suspect | [27] that, at least at the larger sanctuaries, the priests had at their disposal formulas which, with a few alterations and insertions, could be used for any occasion at all, as seems to have been the case in Assyria.[43] The great variety in form that we now find in the songs was perhaps only introduced after the separation from the cult, and it is possible that other elements, such as the lament about persecutions, did not find their way in until then.

It now becomes clear, too, why the songs are, in general, so unspecific[44] and why we can in fact deduce so little from them

# Chapter 3

## JEREMIAH'S POEMS OF LAMENT[1]

### 1. *11.18-20, 21-23*

*Verse 18*. The 'and' that opens the verse in the MT is to be deleted, with GS; this was intended to facilitate the transition from what came before, with which there was originally no connection at all.—For הראיתני, G reads ראיתי, which deserves preference as far as both content and metre are concerned (Cornill, Erbt, Rothstein).

*Verse 19* ולא ידעתי כי sounds prosaic, and ו and כי are missing in G. Since the second line of v. 19 evidently begins with עלי, those words are to be taken with the first line and refer to the lamb. I then read לא יָדַע (Cornill). When G reads לאמר לכו ו (similarly, SV) after מחשבות, on metrical grounds alone this can only be a fill-in (against Giesebrecht). Following Hitzig, almost all more recent scholars read בְּלֵחוֹ for בלחמו which is inexplicable in this context. Ehrlich, following G reads נשיתה for נשחיתה and with ST understands עץ as 'poison', for which there is however no attestation. Occasionally wood, from a tree that has been struck by lightning, for example, or from a hollow in a tree, serves as a magical implement (cf. Ad. Wuttke, *Der deutsche Volksglaube in der Gegenwart* [Popular German Belief in the Present Day], 3rd edn by E.H. Meyer [1900], § 121, p. 97), so that it could be that ST are right after all. I delete the ו in front of נכרתנו—which should probably be pointed as a hiphil (Keil, Ehrlich)—as being at least superfluous in the transition from the metaphor to the application.

*Verse 20*. The ו at the | [29] beginning of the verse is missing in G, present in SV, and is indispensable on account of the contrast to what comes before. צבאות is to be deleted, following G. For the meaningless גליתי I read, with Cornill, Duhm and others, גַלּוֹתִי, following Pss. 22.9[8]; 37.5; Prov. 16.3, and then עליך instead of אליך, following Ps. 37.5. The את before ריבי can be dispensed with (Budde).

*Verse 21*. Since a new song clearly commences at v. 21 (see below), I delete לכן as a redactional link; following G I read נפש and יָדֵינו.

*Verse 22*. The first five words which introduce the divine speech are to be deleted (so, most recent scholars). הבחורים and בניהם appear to be variants. Since בחורים is never found with בנות but always with בתולות, בניהם must be taken as the original reading. Perhaps the text should be rearranged to

בחרב ימותו: the present position may have been caused by the insertion of
הבחורים. The single instance of ימותו, should perhaps be replaced by יתמו
(Hitzig, Ewald).

*Verse 23*. With GSV, על should be written for אל. Verse 23a I join directly
to v. 22a.

| 18 | Yahweh made it known to me; then I knew; | |
| | then I saw their deeds. | (3 + 3) |
| 19 | But I was like a gentle lamb | |
| | that is led to the slaughter, suspecting nothing; | (3 + 3) |
| | Against me they devised schemes: | |
| | 'Let us destroy the tree in its sap | (3 + 3) |
| | Let us cut him off from the land of the living | |
| | that his name be remembered no more' | (3 + 3) |
| 20 | But Yahweh judges righteously, | |
| | he tries reins and heart. | (3 + 3) |
| | I shall see thy vengeance upon them, | |
| | for to thee I committed my cause. | (3 + 3) |

| 21 | Thus says Yahweh concerning the men of Anathoth, | |
| | who sought after my life, saying: | |
| | 'You must not prophesy in Yahweh's name, | |
| | or you will die by our hand'. | (3 + 3) |
| 22a | Yes, I shall punish them | |
| 23a | and no issue shall remain to them. | (3 + 3) |
| 22b | Their sons shall fall by the sword, | |
| | their daughters shall die by famine; | (3 + 3) |
| 23b | For I will bring evil | |
| | upon Anathoth's men | |
| | in the year of their punishment'. | (6) |

Two pieces that are closely related in content stand together here.[2]
The first consists of six double trimeters, two of which in each case
together form a strophe. The second is constructed somewhat more
irregularly. | [30] If לאמר is deleted, v. 21a could easily be measured as
a six-feet verse (Erbt); but since it is simply the introduction to the
following divine word, which usually, as narrative, bears a prosaic
form, this will just be a case of rhythmic prose.

The first song immediately gets off to a powerful start. Yahweh has
opened the prophet's eyes, so that he has become aware of the
dangerous goings-on around him. How this happened is not said.
Perhaps through a special revelation. Or perhaps by perfectly natural
means, through a conversation, maybe, that he just happened to

overhear. Then Jeremiah would have seen this as a special act of
providence, in just the same way as he later attributes the chance
visit to the potter—which suddenly releases in him a new and
important realization—to a particular command of Yahweh (18.1ff.);[3]
or as he sees the word of Yahweh in the fact that his cousin offers to
sell him the field (32.8); or as Hosea, in retrospect, presents his
marriage to a woman who later proves unfaithful as being willed and
ordered by Yahweh. In any case, however it came about, the secret,
heavenly communication betrays the prophet; for he alone stands on
such an intimate footing and is accustomed to receiving all kinds of
secret and confidential communications. Such a feature is quite
unthinkable in the Psalms; for the oracle that occasionally occurs
there[4] is limited to the expression of the petition's being heard and
accepted, and thus parallels the 'assurance of being heard'.

The verse that follows shifts back to the situation prior to the first
verse to picture the prophet as he was before that warning. He
compares himself to a docile lamb which naïvely follows the person
who is taking it to be slaughtered—a moving image! In the same way,
Jeremiah has previously thought his own folk capable only of kind
and good things, and now he is so bitterly disillusioned!

The lamb, for the Israelite, is one of the animals most frequently
offered in sacrifices. Cornill points out that in no fewer than 111 of
the 116 OT passages that speak of the כבש, the reference is to a
sacrifice. We find the sheep or lamb used in this sense a number of
times in the Psalms.

> Thou hast made us like sheep for slaughter . . .
> We are accounted as sheep for the slaughter,

says the communal psalm of lament, Ps. 44.12, 23[11, 22]; cf. also Ps.
49.15[14] (where the text is uncertain, however), and Jer. 12.3.
Unlike such passages as these, ours lays special emphasis on the
animal's trust and innocence. | [31] The image is used differently
again in Isa. 53.7, where the emphasis lies on the mute suffering of
the sheep. The two last-mentioned passages thus mean an inten-
sification of the usual image, but in a slightly different direction in
each case. If the Jeremiah passage is accepted as authentic, it could
well seem likely that the passage in Deutero-Isaiah is dependent
upon our passage, but this cannot be proven. It is of course even less
easy to prove the reverse, that our passage is a quotation from that
one, as Hölscher maintains.

This poignant self-description could easily find a place in a psalm of lament, and indeed the next line, which speaks of his opponents' secret plans, leads us right into this realm; cf. above, p. 25 and Pss. 10.2; 21.12[11]; 35.4; 41.8[7]; 56.6[5]; 64.7[6]; 140.3, 5[2, 4]; the agreement generally extends as far as the word חשב (מחשבה 56.6[5]). The verbatim citation of the evil plan also has its counterpart there (71.11; 74.8). And the last line of v. 19 reappears almost word for word in a communal song of lament (Ps. 83.5[4]).

With v. 20 a new idea is introduced. The 'and Yahweh' corresponds to the 'and I' in v. 19, marking the transition to another idea, as often in the Psalms (cf. Pss. 22.4, 7, (10) 20[3, 6, (9) 19]; 59.6, 9, 17[5, 8, 16]; 69.6,[5] 14, 20, 30[5, 13, 19, 29]). In the face of the evil that his own relatives and friends think him guilty of, and of the malice that they are planning against him, Jeremiah has a strong source of comfort: however much people misunderstand and persecute him, the divine Judge exercises justice and is not deceived by appearances; he looks into the heart! Both ideas belong to the song of lament (with v. 20aα, cf. Ps. 7.12[11]; 119.75; with v. 20aβ, particularly for בחן, Pss. 7.10[9]; 17.3[2]; 26.2[1]); the latter idea belongs to the motif of trust and innocence.

Driver, Erbt and Rothstein follow G, where 'and' is absent and Yahweh appears in the vocative. But the parallels in the Psalms (e.g. Ps. 7.10-12[9-11]) show that v. 20a is to be taken on its own; the alternation between second and third person does not tell against this, for it is a common phenomenon (cf. Pss. 3.4-9[3-8]; 7.9[8]; 12.2-4, 7f.[1-3, 6f.]; 13.5f.; 16.1f., 5-11; 25.10f., 15f.; 26.11f.; 28.4-6, 8f. etc.). But as a just and unerring judge, Yahweh sees not only the innocence of the persecuted one but also the guilt of the persecutor. This idea leads on to the next line. Jeremiah is certain that they will have their punishment. The אראה can be seen as a petition, 'may I see', or better as an expression of assurance, since the psalms of lament do often conclude with such certainty.

The passionate desire for revenge creates difficulties for exegetes. | [32] The preference is to interpret the desire as being not for personal revenge but for Yahweh's cause. But the wording gives no indication of this; נקמתך simply says: the vengeance that comes from thee; cf. נקמתי in Ezek. 25.14, 17, also משפטי in Ezek. 39.21, משפטו in Zeph. 3.5. It is still a wish that we find distasteful.[6] And yet, may we not often have too gentle and spiritual a view of the prophet? Beneath his mild disposition there lies dormant the heated temperament of the oriental; when this flares up at any time, beware! The fact that in the song of lament the petition against the enemy, and even the curse, is no rarity,[7] may go some way towards excusing Jeremiah. The petition is supported by an expression of trust, with which we are also acquainted from there (Ps. 22.9[8]; 37.5; Prov. 16.3; cf. p. 23).

The song concludes on this note. In the main its outline is that of the song of lament: v. 19, first of all the innocence motif, then a piece from the lament; 20a, innocence and trust motif; 20b, petition for vengeance. Only v. 18, the warning, is extrinsic to the scheme and has no parallel there; here the prophet has left his tell-tale mark.

The structure of the second song is quite different. Here, following v. 21, which has been prefixed as an introduction, there comes a divine word which presents the men of Anathoth with the prospect of severe punishment, even total annihilation, for their persecution of Jeremiah. The sword will destroy the pugnacious young men, and hunger will kill those who stay at home (cf. Lam. 1.20).[8] It is his home town that Jeremiah is threatening with this! A terrible message, especially considering the strong love for home that people of antiquity had. What raging anger must have filled the prophet when he spoke these words!

The authenticity of the passage has been called into question a number of times.[9] Its authenticity, however, is indicated above all by the mention of Anathoth, which is certainly not due simply to speculation and deduction. The most that can be claimed in this regard is that the saying has come down to us in a secondarily expanded form, as Cornill and Erbt in particular presume. Meanwhile I see no cause for further deletions in vv. 22f. beyond those suggested above. The saying could certainly have been shorter, but its present form may just as well be its original one. The 'year of their punishment' is an eschatological term; Yahweh is presented as a great king who from time to time | [33] holds a review of his lands;[10] cf. 8.12 (and following this, 6.15); 23.12.

The passage is usually taken simply as the continuation and conclusion of the preceding one. But the verbose introduction in v. 21a and the justification in v. 21b, which is incompatible with v. 19—in the latter, secret assassination plans, in the former an open threat—make it much more likely that vv. 21-23 comprise an independent piece,[11] for otherwise it is difficult to see why such a superfluous and thoroughly unfitting motivation should have been added. The originally completely independent passages were then juxtaposed because the situation is similar in both cases, and perhaps the second was intended as an answer to the first, as is the case elsewhere.

As a result of this division, the first song does lose its only concrete datum, namely the mention of his home town, which would have been so valuable for our understanding of him. In particular we should like to know why Jeremiah was persecuted. Some have related it to his activity on behalf of Deuteronomy (11.1-14);[12] but even supposing that section is genuine—which is hotly disputed—it does not, in any case, have any direct connection with our song. It could just as easily be that Jeremiah's annunciation of disaster aroused the people's displeasure,[13] as may be presupposed by the second song (v. 21b).

Unlike the first song, the second is purely prophetic in form: a divine word with its introduction. Essentially it does not belong to the 'poems of lament' at all; it is treated here with these only because of its relatedness in terms of situation and ideas.

## 2. 15.15-21

*Verse 15.* The words אתה ידעת are missing in G, but in terms of content and metre fit the context well. The sentence אל לארך אפך תקחני presents difficulties. The translation 'In thy forbearance (towards my enemies) take me not away' is not very probable, because one then has to imagine what it is referring to. If לארך אפך were reliable, one could read תִּנָּקֵם instead of תקחני (Gunkel); but then one should expect לְאֶרֶךְ אַפֶּיךָ. Duhm's emendation to אַל־תַּאֲרֵךְ is attractive. It is less easy to follow Duhm in his deletion of תקחני, even though it is absent in G. Rather, I would suggest וְנַקֵּנִי; an explanation for its omission in G would be that | [34] it slipped in by mistake just before, in place of הנקם לי.

*Verse 16.* With Duhm I read מִנֹּאֲצֵי and כֻלָּם, and vocalize further as וַיְהִי with Duhm, Cornill and Erbt. In my line divisions I follow Erbt, who, however, needlessly has a new poem begin at v. 16b. For the second דבריך the singular should be read, following GSV, and thus in the first occurrence also. אלהי צבאות is metrically superfluous and is to be deleted.

*Verse 18.* There is no need to depart from MT in favour of G in aα. The deletion of מאנה הרפא (Rothstein, H. Schmidt) is hardly justified.

*Verse 19.* The whole introduction is external to the metre. Before לפני I add a וֹ, with GS (Rothstein). Verse 19b lacks colour and anticipates v. 20 and should therefore be deleted (Cornill, Duhm).

*Verses 20f.* seem to have been contaminated with 1.18f. I thus delete v. 20aβ as encroachments from there.

| | | |
|---|---|---:|
| 15 | Thou knowest, Yahweh; | |
| | think of me and take my part. | (5) |
| | Take vengeance for me on my persecutors, | |
| | do not put off thy anger, and acquit me. | (3 + 3) |
| | Know that for thy sake | |
| | I bear reproach | |
| 16 | from those who despise thy word. | (6) |
| | Destroy them, then thy word | |
| | will be my delight and the joy of my heart. | (3 + 3) |
| | Because thy name, Yahweh, I bear, | |
| 17 | I do not sit in the company of merry-makers, rejoicing. | (4 + 4) |
| | Under thy hand | |
| | I sit alone; | |
| | for thou hast filled me with indignation. | (6) |
| 18 | Why then has my pain become unceasing, | |
| | my wound incurable, refusing to heal? | (4 + 4) |
| | Yes, thou becamest a deceitful brook to me, | |
| | waters that fail!— | (6) |
| 19 | Thereupon Yahweh answered me thus: | |
| | 'If you return, I will return you, | |
| | and you shall stand before me. | (5) |
| | If you bring forth[14] what is precious, with nothing worthless, | |
| | you shall be my mouthpiece. | (5) |
| 20 | Then I will make you for this people | |
| | a steep wall of bronze. | (3 + 3) |
| 21 | And I will deliver you out of the hand of the wicked | |
| | and redeem you from the grasp of the ruthless'. | (3 + 3) |

| [35] The song of lament style is evident right from the beginning. The 'thou knowest' with which Jeremiah points to his miserable situation is found also in the Psalms absolutely, as in our passage, in Ps. 40.9, with object in Pss. 31.8[7]; 69.20[19]; 142.4[3]. You must know, Jeremiah is saying, how things are, through no fault of my own; so remember me and do not take your hand from me! This petition also comes from the song of lament (cf. Ps. 106.4, also 8.4; זכר on its own in Pss. 25.6f.; 74.2, 18, 22; 89.48, 51[47, 50], פקד on its own in 80.15[14]). It is linked to the passionate desire for revenge, as in 11.20 and 12.3. If the Hebrew text is reliable, Jeremiah is not asking 'avenge me', as the Greek translation may suppose,[15] but

'avenge thyself for me', which is influenced by the idea, expressed openly later on, that Yahweh's honour is also at stake and that his enemies are Yahweh's enemies too.[16] The enemies are more often mentioned in the psalms of lament (Pss. 7.2[1]; 35.3; 119.157).

There is also another reason for Yahweh to intervene at once: if he hesitates, it will be all up with his loyal servant. And after all it is for Yahweh that he is suffering so much reproach (cf. Ps. 69.8, 10[7, 9]) from those who despise Yahweh's word (cf. 23.17;[17] Pss. 10.3, 13; 74.10, 18). The savage request for revenge is repeated (for כלה cf. Pss. 59.14[13]; 74.11); only then will he be able to rejoice at Yahweh's word. Here one might at first be unsure whether 'God's word' should be understood as Yahweh's commandment in the sense of Ps. 119 (Hölscher), or as the divine word that has come to the prophet. As v. 17b will show, we should assume the latter. According to the text as it has come down to us, v. 16aβ would refer to the past: thy word was my delight and joy—a renewed declaration of innocence which would stand in effective contrast to those who despise God's word.[18] But this is contradicted by the fact that Jeremiah only reluctantly became a prophet and later also saw his prophetic compulsion always as a crippling burden (Duhm, Cornill). And even if there were perhaps moments in his life when he thought differently and was proud to have the privilege of being Yahweh's prophet, in the mood that gave rise to our song (cf. especially v. 17), he thinks only of how much he has already had to bear for that privilege. So it will be better to relate the words to the future, simply changing the vocalization: He would so love to be able to enjoy God's word, and longs for a time when he will be able to do so without having at the same time to suffer so terribly. A religious motif has been mixed into that | [36] unrestrainedly hateful petition, which is able to mitigate it a little.[19] Jeremiah is groping for a way out of the darkness that surrounds him. But the recognition that true happiness usually grows only out of suffering is still hidden from him.

From his brief look into the future he returns to the present. It is because he is Yahweh's property and bears his name[20]—perhaps there is also an allusion to the name Jeremiah (H. Schmidt)—that he is so lonely and cheerless. Verse 17a reminds us of that passage in the song of lament where the psalmist maintains that he has avoided the society of the wicked and ungodly (Ps. 26.4f.; cf. 1.1). But here it is a matter of far more innocuous company: he has never sat in the company of the merry-makers, has never joined in the gay social life.

That motif has thus taken on a quite special hue here. In it lies a reproach, a quiet complaint about lost happiness. It follows from these words that Jeremiah is by nature a cheerful person who enjoys company and friendship. The separation that the psalmist insists on, Jeremiah can only see as a burdensome curse on him. Long since, Yahweh has required him to give up house and home (12.6), the love of a woman and the joy of fatherhood (16.1ff.), and when for once he does try to mix in happy society, then horrific images arise before him and he sees those who now are so merry, lying there as corpses (cf. 4.19-21; 10.19ff.; 14.18), so that even this joy is turned sour on him.[21] Small wonder if for once he opens his silent mouth and his long-suppressed yearning for a life like everyone else's is heard.

Verse 17b, too, is still dominated by this gloomy mood: on account of 'Yahweh's hand' he has to sit alone. This expression is used to indicate the dark urge that irresistibly overwhelms the prophet and presses him against his will into Yahweh's service (Isa. 8.11; Ezek. 1.3; 3.14, 22; 8.1; 33.22; 37.1; 40.1; 1 Kgs 18.46; 2 Kgs 3.15). Hölscher,[22] who (on p. 24 of his book) himself cites the passages just mentioned, prefers | [37] to understand the expression differently, namely in line with its usage in cases of sickness or other misfortune, where Yahweh's hand is said to rest on one or smite one (Pss. 32.4; 38.3[2]; 39.11[10]). Telling against this is, firstly, the fact that in v. 16b, the corresponding member of the parallel line, there is no mention of such a lament; furthermore, that the expression understood in Hölscher's sense could only have a place in the lament, not in the innocence motif, which is really the only way to view v. 17. Finally, the זעם that occurs in the same connection always denotes the divine wrath, expressed in a context of judgment (Isa. 10.5, 25; 13.5; 26.20; 30.27; Jer. 10.10; 50.25; Ezek. 21.31; 22.24, 31; Nah. 1.6; Hab. 3.12; Zeph. 3.8; Pss. 38.4[3]; 69.25[24]; 78.49; 102.11[10]; Lam. 2.6; Dan. 8.19; 11.36).[23] The sense, then, is: Jeremiah is filled with an anger that Yahweh himself has instilled in him.[24] The inner ardour that takes hold of him again and again, making him incapable of joining any kind of merry company, comes—he is convinced—from the deity himself. He expresses himself similarly in 6.11: I am filled with Yahweh's anger.[25] Clearly, a prophet is speaking here too.

In v. 18 the lament[26] style is unmistakable. I need only refer to the instances of למה (cf. p. 27), נצח[27] (Pss. 13.2; 44.24; 74.1, 3, 10, 19; 77.9; 79.5; 89.47[46]) and כאב (Ps. 39.3[2]). The terms 'pain' and 'blow' really refer to physical suffering; here they are used metaphorically for mental anguish, the cleft in his soul created by the dichotomy between divine compulsion and human desire.

The next line even carries a severe reproach against Yahweh, which should not be tempered by changing the text into a question.[28] Yahweh |[38] has let him down like a 'brook of lies', like a watercourse that one counts on in a long walk through the wilderness only to find it dried up (Job 6.15-20).[29] For Yahweh's sake he has done without so much, has accepted so much hardship; but Yahweh's help has failed to materialize, he has not kept his word: he cannot be relied upon! The prophet is here speaking with his God as a faithful servant, disgruntled with his master, might dare to speak his mind, while the master, acknowledging the servant's loyalty thus far, does not take it amiss.

Here, at the point when the lament has reached its climax, on the brink of utter despair, comes Yahweh's answer. But, as in 12.5f., this turns out to be quite different from what one might have expected. Not a word of recognition and comfort. If Jeremiah 'returns', he too will 'return' him (the same word-play as in 31.18b)—it is intentional that the oracle initially sounds obscure and incomprehensible, and becomes only gradually more comprehensible.[30] Jeremiah's last words thus meant a falling-away from Yahweh, a revolt against his service. עמד לפני is the term for serving, waiting upon a superior. Hölscher understands it here, as in 18.20, to refer to standing before Yahweh in the temple with thank-offering and votive offering (1 Kgs 3.15). More frequently, however, it is used of the prophet (1 Kgs 17.1; 18.15; 2 Kgs 3.14; 5.16). That this is the only possible sense here is demonstrated by the parallel כפי תהיה. Understanding it as he does, though, Hölscher has to find this expression 'strange'; but in reference to the prophet it is perfectly clear (cf. 1.9; 5.14, 'I put my words in your mouth'; 4.15f.; 7.1; Isa. 51.16; 59.21).[31]

So to begin with Yahweh promises him nothing, except that he may continue to exercise his prophetic office. This service, which brings him so much pain, he 'may' continue with! His profession, with all its sorrows, is still his most cherished privilege! There is one condition, it is true: the mouth that proclaims the divine words must not, alongside what is 'precious', also utter the 'worthless', human laments and petitions! The form and content of the verse—the deeper understanding that he has finally come to, after a long inner struggle, dressed as a divine speech—are strongly reminiscent of 12.5f.

There does then follow an eventual | [39] promise (vv. 20f.),[32] which should at least make his service a little easier: 'You will not be defeated by your enemies, even should the whole nation assail you; for I am with you'. But the promise relates only to this one, albeit most important, point, that Yahweh will not let him down. The other matters he has complained about are not answered at all: the deity has no ear for his pains and petitions; nothing is going to change there! Jeremiah now realizes that the way of the prophet means giving up all earthly happiness; he has to be content with that one certainty. The result is similar to that in 12.6; as there, renunciation of joy and happiness. But a feature that is missing there is added here, so that the prospects are not so bleak after all.

As in v. 19, the prophet has left his mark in v. 20 also—he alone can be called a wall against the people (1.18; 15.12). The psalms style does not reappear, it seems, until close to the end; cf. עריצים[33] (Pss. 54.5; 86.14; Prov. 11.16; Job 6.23; 27.13). Jeremiah is thinking especially of those who seek after his life, Jehoiakim and his mighty men, perhaps (Duhm). However, there are so many possible situations in his life in which such a word could be placed that it will be better to refrain from any attempt to fix it chronologically. Erbt's supposition (pp. 179f.), that the song derives from the time when Jeremiah had to hide from Jehoiakim, is to be rejected. His 'sitting alone' has, as we have seen, reasons quite other than the political circumstances.

In the case of this song, Hölscher also has to admit that the conclusion has been 'adapted to fit Jeremiah'. I think I have shown that the reference to the prophet permeates the whole of the song.[34] The structure is as follows: vv. 15, 16a, petition with motif; vv. 16b-18 lament (v. 17 actually innocence motif, but re-formed as a lament); vv. 19-21 answer in the form of a divine speech. The dependence on the outline of the song of lament is clear. | [40] The prophet's point of view is evident outwardly in the form of the divine speech, and in content in vv. 16, 17, 19, 20. The passionate reproach of v. 18b, also, would be scarcely conceivable in the Psalms.

### 3. *17.12-18*

*Verse 13.* For יסורי read וְסוּרֶיךָ, following TV (Ewald, Giesebrecht). לארץ should replace בארץ (Gunkel); as in Exod. 15.12; Jon. 2.7; Pss. 22; 71; 143; Sir. 51.9, ארץ here denotes the underworld (cf. Gunkel, *Ausgewählte Psalmen* [3rd edn], p. 340). For the whole expression, cf. כל־הכתוב לחיים in Isa. 4.3.

מים is to be deleted, following G (Rothstein). את־יהוה is a gloss, which actually belongs at the end of v. 14 as אתה יהוה (Duhm).

*Verse 14.* From the gloss at the end of v. 13 I insert יהוה after the אתה, so that we obtain a single trimeter.

*Verse 16.* For מרעה, incomprehensible in its present vocalization, most recent scholars, following the lead of J.D. Michaelis, read מֵרָעָה, with S, and translate: 'I have not pressed you because of the evil'. Attractive though this is, it founders on the fact that מן, 'because of', can only refer to something at hand or past, not to something that has yet to come in the future. One would at least have to amend to לרעה. But it is simpler to amend to יום רעה, which is then, as an accusative, dependent on אצתי, which seems possible in view of Exod. 5.13. I do not see how metrical considerations are supposed to tell against this (Cornill). אחריך then means 'behind your back', to which נכח פניך corresponds. אתה ידעת I take with the second half of the verse for the sake of the metre.

| | | |
|---|---|---|
| 12 | Throne of glory, | |
| | High-place from the beginning, | |
| | place of our sanctuary, | (6) |
| 13 | Hope of Israel, Yahweh! | |
| | All will be put to shame who forsake thee, | (3 + 3) |
| | Those who turn away from thee will be ascribed to Sheol; | |
| | for they have forsaken the fount of life. | (3 + 3) |
| 14 | Heal me, Yahweh, and I shall be healed, | |
| | help me, and I shall be helped. | (3 + 3) |
| | For my praise art thou, Yahweh. | (3) |
| 15 | Behold, they say to me: | |
| | 'where is Yahweh's word? Let it come!' | (4 + 4) |
| 16 | But I did not pursue behind thy back the day of disaster, | |
| | and the evil day I did not wish for. | (4 + 4) |
| | Thou thyself knowest what came through my lips; | |
| | it lay open before thee. | (7) |
| 17 | Be thou not a disappointment to me, | |
| | thou my confidence on the day of disaster! | (7) |
| | \| [41] | |
| 18 | Put to shame may my persecutors be, not I put to shame; | |
| | may they be disappointed, not I disappointed! | (4 + 4) |
| | Bring upon them the day of disaster | |
| | and smash them utterly to pieces! | (3 + 3) |

The song begins with a festive, hymnic introduction (vv. 12f.), a string of honorific titles for the temple and Yahweh,[36] which Graf already took, correctly, as vocatives, while more recent scholars endeavour to distinguish subject and predicate. The linking up of so many words gives the address the tone of fervent calling. Following this is a statement about those who have backslidden from Yahweh, which also amounts to a praise of Yahweh; it belongs to God's honour that there is no life, no existence, without him (cf. Pss. 104.27-30; 145.15f.). Of the songs of lament in the Psalter, only one has a hymnic introduction (80.2f.[1f.]); examples are more numerous elsewhere: Neh. 1.5ff.; 9.6ff.; Dan. 9.4ff.; also the prayer of Manasseh, Azariah and Mordecai, *2 Bar.* 48.2ff.; *Pss. Sol.* 5, 17; *4 Ezra* 8.20ff. Though these examples are all late, the custom will also be an old one; for the Babylonian-Assyrian songs of lament often have a hymnic introduction.[37] It seems such a natural thing to do to first glorify the deity from whom one wants to request something, thus putting him in a favourable mood. In the same way, the communal song of lament Jer. 14.2-9 contains in v. 8 a hymnic invocation of Yahweh.

These two verses are now usually considered inauthentic,[38] even in the view of such scholars as think the following song authentic.[39] The reasons adduced for this are, however, for the most part very unconvincing. It is wrong to see in these verses a 'mosaic of borrowed expressions'. The fact that so many parallels to the various expressions can be pointed to, some from the book of Jeremiah itself, can be simply explained by the fact that some of them are titles of honour taken from cultic language,[40] while others are expressions that are common elsewhere. To consider literary dependence or borrowing at this point is quite misguided. Thus it is also completely immaterial whether such parallels within the book of Jeremiah are authentic or not. The antiquity of the verses is scarcely open to question. When Giesebrecht sees in 'high-place from the beginning' a sign of post-exilic composition, since there would have been considerably older sanctuaries in pre-exilic times, | [42] he is forgetting that the pious worshipper can easily call a sanctuary that has existed for over 300 years 'ancient', even if others are still older. Religious piety likes to think that its objects are ancient. Another question is whether these verses could conceivably come from a prophet who speaks out so scathingly against the temple (chs. 7; 26). They do indeed contradict those words, but it is, psychologically, understandable enough if the same Jeremiah in a moment of need kneels in the temple like a poor sick person and beseeches Yahweh with such words: now the prophet is in need of comfort and help himself! And so the words may still be authentic.[41]

The song of lament proper begins immediately with the petition. The cry 'heal me', which strictly speaking presupposes illness, is known to us from the Psalms (Pss. 6.3[2]; 41.5[4]; 60.4[2]; cf. 30.3[2]; 107.20). The more general 'help me' is even more common (Pss. 3.8[7]; 6.5[4]; 7.2[1]; 22.22[21]; 31.17; 54.3[1]; 59.3[2]; 69.2[1]; 71.2; 109.26; 119.94, 146). 'My praise art thou' (cf. Pss. 71.6; 109.1) is doubly appropriate when it is preceded by the hymnic introduction.[42]

The lament begins at v. 15. The prophet turns to his enemies and points to them—as if wagging his finger; he makes use of the well-known form whereby the speech of the ungodly is cited verbatim.[43] In a significant way, however, our passage differs from corresponding ones in the Psalms. There, Yahweh's world rule is subjected to doubt, here the coming of his word is mockingly called for—clear evidence that we are dealing with a prophet here. The same reproach is made against Isaiah (5.19; cf. 28.23ff.) and indeed no prophet seems to have escaped it. Duhm deletes v. 15 as an interpolation following Isa. 5.19, since he cannot reconcile it with the accusation presupposed in v. 16.[44] The strongly divergent wording of the passage alone makes such a borrowing unlikely. Verse 16 would then be up in the air, too; the protestation of innocence requires a charge. The relation between v. 15 and v. 16 is in fact quite obvious. The people mock him because his prophecy is not fulfilled. As if he himself would take pleasure in or have an interest in its being fulfilled! They have no idea | [43] how hard he finds it to make such prophecies of disaster. For him, then, there is no doubt at all that the word will come; he therefore does not begin to answer that reproach. What wounds him is the complete misunderstanding of his nature. How can people abuse their best friend, the tireless petitioner of his people, as if he were Israel's evil enemy! Truly, Yahweh, who has heard his ardent prayers, knows better.

Verse 16 is an innocence motif but bears the mark of the prophet in its content. Verse 16a would be unthinkable in a psalm. And even v. 16b, which could in fact have a place in a psalm (cf. Ps. 139.4, מוצא שפתי, Ps. 89.35[34]), is given a special sense in this context: Yahweh knows that he has never expressed such a demand, and that he is no 'malicious magus'.

In his distress Jeremiah turns to Yahweh and expresses to him his trust (cf. Pss. 62.8[7]; 71.7; 91.2, 9; 142.6[5]), but at the same time, impressed by the incessant mockery to which he is exposed, the desire to stand vindicated at last before the world. On בוש cf. above, p. 27, and Pss. 31.18[17]; 35.4; 40.15; 70.3[2], חתת, which never occurs in the Psalms, has a similar meaning (Ehrlich). On רדפי, cf. 15.15 (pp. 46f.).

Certainly his petition stands in contradiction to his earlier behaviour, to which he has only just appealed. But it is not such a contradiction as to warrant the deletion of v. 18 (Cornill, Duhm).[45] Though he categorically rejects that accusation with regard to the past, now he finally loses his patience and does what he has just denied doing. The day of disaster, which formerly he wanted to avert by his petitioning, he, himself, now wishes for! Morally speaking this may be open to objection, but psychologically it is quite understandable. We find something similar in the Psalter: the psalmist first maintains that he has shown his enemies nothing but good (35.12-14; 109.5) and immediately afterwards he showers them with the most dreadful maledictions (35.22-26; 109.6-20).[46]

The song of lament outline stands out clearly again here: v. 14, petition; v. 15, lament (speech of the ungodly); v. 16, innocence motif; v. 17, petition and trust motif; v. 18, petition and curse. The prophetic point of view is evident in v. 15 and v. 16a.

In the same chapter as this song, only a few verses earlier, we find two verses to which we must briefly turn our attention, namely 17.9f. | [44]

> Deep[47] is the heart and[48] evil.
>> Who could fathom it out?                    (5)
> I, Yahweh, search the heart
>> and[49] try the reins.[50]                   (5)

A dialogue between man and God is usually seen in this passage. First, the lament over the weakness, unfathomability and unpredictability of the human heart, in which there are echoes of a gloomy personal experience (Cornill, Duhm). The words put into Yahweh's mouth as an answer are known to us from 11.20. There—on the lips of the man at prayer—they are an expression of trust, while here—on Yahweh's lips—they are intended to bring comfort.

Now Cornill and Duhm want to place this fragment—for clearly this is what it is—before v. 14: after Jeremiah has been given the comforting answer of v. 10a he dares to make that request. But this conflicts with the song of lament style. The divine answer guarantees that he has been heard and thereby marks the conclusion of the song. At v. 12 (or v. 14) a new piece begins, new in both content and form. There is nothing at all to suggest that anything preceded it. One might rather be tempted to see in vv. 9f. the conclusion to vv. 14–18.[51] Then v. 9a would also be spoken by Yahweh and it would be better to keep the עקב found in the tradition. This answer meant a gentle refusal of the overly impetuous request, and at the same time the assurance that Yahweh sees beyond the unpleasant desire for revenge into the depths of his heart and thus does not charge this over-enthusiasm too heavily to his account. In 12.5f. and 15.19ff., however, the refusal is much sharper, the whole answer deeper and more original. It will thus be better to take vv. 9f. on their own, or, better, as a fragment removed from a lost context. The psalms-style is unmistakable; there is nothing prophetic in it, so that in view of its limited length no certain conclusions can be drawn concerning its authenticity either.

## 4. *18.18-23*

*Verse 18.* ויאמרו is extrinsic to the metre and may simply be a make-shift connection. For מחשבות I read the singular, following GS. The אל, deleted by most recent scholars, I retain.

*Verse 19.* Instead of יְרִיבַי (Caspari, Cornill, Duhm, | [45] Erbt, Rothstein, H. Schmidt, Staerk, following MT) I read רִיבִי, following GS (Giesebrecht, Ehrlich). The parallelism of v. 19a in particular supports this; otherwise one is forced to understand שמע differently from הקשיבה, which is why Duhm deletes אלי, while H. Schmidt emends it to אליהם, which runs counter to the style of the songs of lament. Though קול ריבי is not attested, it is just as possible as קול שועי in Ps. 5.3[2], or קול תחנוני as in Pss. 28.2; 31.23[22]; 130.2; cf. p. 30.

*Verse 20aβ* resists the line division and anticipates v. 22b, and should thus be deleted as an intruding interpolation from v. 22, found in a more expanded form in G (Giesebrecht).

*Verse 21.* The verse is very overcrowded. I delete לכן, the ו in front of תהינה (GSV), ואלמנות (Rothstein), יהיו and the whole of b (Giesebrecht, Rothstein).

*Verse 22.* I delete עליהם, which is more readily dispensable than פתאם (against Rothstein).

*Verse 23.* I delete כל for metrical reasons and read תמח ויהיו (Erbt). In b, read with Cornill, following G, יְהִי מֻכְשָׁלִם, 'their offence be before you', which gives a better parallelism with the following line; in substance, this is reminiscent of how Dareios has a servant admonish him daily during his

meal, with the words 'Lord, remember the Athenians!' (Herodotus 5.105).—
Instead of בהם, בם should be read, for the sake of the metre.

| | | |
|---|---|---|
| 18 | And they said: | |
| | 'Come, let us make an attack on Jeremiah | (4) |
| | For the Law will not let the priest down, | |
| | nor counsel the wise man, nor the word the prophet. | (4 + 4) |
| | Come, let us smite him with the tongue | |
| | and let us not heed all of his words!' | (3 + 3) |
| 19 | Give heed, Yahweh, to me | |
| | and hear the voice of my right. | (3 + 3) |
| 20 | May one recompense good with evil? | |
| | Remember how I stood before thee, | (3 + 3) |
| | To speak for their good, | |
| | to turn thine anger from them. | (3 + 3) |
| 21 | Give up their sons to hunger, | |
| | deliver them into the hands of the sword! | (3 + 3) |
| | Let their wives lose their children | |
| | and may their men meet death by pestilence! | (3 + 3) |
| 22 | May crying be heard from their houses | |
| | when thou bringest suddenly the marauding host! | (3 + 3) |
| | For they dug a pit to catch me | |
| | and for my feet they laid snares. | (3 + 3) |
| 23 | Yet thou, Yahweh, knowest | |
| | what they are plotting, to kill me. | (3 + 3) |
| | Forgive them not their sin, | |
| | nor blot out their iniquity before thee; | (3 + 3) |
| | May they always be to thee an offence, | |
| | in the time of thy wrath deal with them! | (3 + 3) |

| [46] The poem begins quite abruptly. The prophet's opponents
have joined forces against him. For comments on the plan of the
ungodly and the use of the expression חשב מחשבה we refer to our
discussion of 11.19 (pp. 43f.).

To understand v. 18aβ, we must bear in mind that in their
speeches the prophets refer to disputes they have had with their
opponents.[52] And just as they occasionally contrast their words to
things their opponents have said, but which are not quoted (Amos
3.2; 9.7; Isa. 7.21ff.; 59.1f.), so here what his opponents say may well
be the reply to his own words.[53] Jeremiah will have said something to
the effect that there is coming a time full of terror and disaster, when
all wisdom will fail and no one will be able to give counsel and help;
then Torah will cease from the priest, counsel from the wise and the

word from the prophet (cf. 4.9; 49.7b; Isa. 29.14b; Ezek. 7.26). They dispute this and maintain the opposite; for this is the way—with simple negation, not with reasons—that they discuss things (cf. Isa. 28.15b, 18f.). The words of v. 18aβ may in fact reflect what they actually said; in v. 18b on the other hand the prophet inserts his own judgment into their speech and has them speak as he thinks they would have to if they were ready to be honest (cf. 2.20, 25; 7.10; Isa. 28.15; Job 21.14). Just as in Ps. 12.4 the words 'with our tongues we are strong' are put on the lips of the ungodly to characterize them, the prophet has his opponents say: 'let us smite him with the tongue'. When they snatch a few of his words out of context and make an accusation out of them, he sees this as lies and slander. And then he has them say: 'let us not heed his words'. He demands that they pay heed to his words, Yahweh's words; but since they do not do so, he thinks they must have agreed this amongst themselves.[54]

Now, however, he turns from the evil designs of his enemies to Yahweh (v. 19). In doing so he deliberately takes up something his opponents have said and reapplies it. If they said 'let us not heed', he now asks 'give them heed'. This הקשיבה is itself derived from the song of lament (Pss. 5.3[2]; 17.1; 55.3[2]; 61.2[1]; 142.7[6]), as is the שמע (Pss. 4.2[1]; 17.1, 6; 27.7; 28.2; 30.11[10]; 39.13[12]; 50.7; 54.4[2]; 61.2[1]; 64.2[1]; 81.9[8]; 84.9[8]; 102.2[1]; 119.149; 130.2[1]; 143.1). It hurts him, that in return for the good that he has shown them he should reap nothing but ingratitude (v. 20). This idea is also found |[47] there (Ps. 35.12; 38.21[20]; 109.5), but with a significant difference. While the psalmist claims to have mourned with them and to have shown them every kindness in other ways (Ps. 35.12-14), Jeremiah here points out—for זכר we refer to 15.15; Pss. 25.6f.; 74.2, 18, 22; 119.49; Lam. 3.19; 5.1—how he has stood before Yahweh[55] and interceded for them.[56] This is only appropriate to a prophet (cf. Gen. 18.23ff.; 20.7, 17 [Abraham], Exod. 8.4, 8f., 24ff.; 10.17f.; 12.32; 32.11ff., 30ff.; Num. 12.13; 14.13ff. [Moses]; 1 Kgs 13.6; 2 Kgs 19.2ff.) and it fits Jeremiah especially well (cf. 7.16; 11.14; 14.11; 15.1f.; 37.3; 42.2).

There now follows a curse over his enemies, one so gruesome that many of our most recent exegetes do not dare to accept that Jeremiah was capable of it. But savagery and passion belong to the prophet's nature: even with Jeremiah, who in many respects is so mild, we find, often enough, eruptions of the most terrible anger.[57] We have no right to turn the angry prophet into a gentle Christian theologian, nor should we expect to find him loving his enemies. Certainly these verses are in no way original; but this is true of many another passage in these songs. When the verses have been purged of the minor additions, there can be no material objection to them.[58] The connection to v. 20 is the best conceivable one.[59] For the apparent contradiction of the claim in v. 20 we refer to our notes on 17.18.[60] That the song should have ended with v. 20 (Cornill, Duhm) is simply out of the question.

After the first curse (vv. 21, 22a) Jeremiah comes back to talking of the persecutions (v. 22b), and describes them with the graphic metaphors from the hunt and birdcatching that are customary in the Psalms (and Proverbs).[61] We meet כרה שוחה in Pss. 57.7[6]; | [48] 119.85, and טמן פח in Pss. 140.6[5]; 142.4[3]. But his consolation is that Yahweh knows all about their plans (v. 23aα). For the ואתה see our remarks on 11.20;[62] for אתה ידעת we refer to 15.15 and the parallels given there.[63] The song closes with a repeated curse (v. 23bβ).

The structure of the whole is clearly that of the song of lament: v. 18, lament (plan of the ungodly); v. 19, petition; v. 20, motif; vv. 21, 22a, curse; v. 22b, lament; v. 23aα, trust motif; v. 23aβ, curse. It is noteworthy how the song begins so very abruptly. In no song of lament in the Psalter do we find anything like this; even when such songs begin straight away with the lament, the first line invariably still contains the divine name (cf. Pss. 3.3[1]; 10.1; 13.2[1]; 22.2[1]; etc.). To begin so abruptly with a speech or a question is prophetic style.[64] That it is a prophet speaking is clear, furthermore, from v. 18aβ and from the reference to intercession (v. 20).

### 5. 20.10-13

*Verse 10.* כי is a redactional link from v. 9. מגור מסביב is a gloss following Ps. 31.14[13] (Erbt, Rothstein, H. Schmidt); see below, p. 61. Following G, the third-person suffix is to be inserted into שלומי. For צלע, 'rib', the figurative meaning, 'side', is not attested in relation to a human being (Cornill), nor would it fit שמר, 'lie in wait', very well either. Since G is no further help on this and the connection of שמר with צלע, 'fall' is difficult, I should like, in the light of Job 13.27; 33.11 and Ps. 56.7[6], where this שמר is linked with ארחות and עקבים, to suggest צעדיו. Read שמרו for שמרי.

*Verse 11.* Read אתי for אותי. One word in 11a is excessive, probably על־כן.

*Verse 12.* = 11.20 and does not fit well after v. 11.

On the classification of *v. 13*, see below. Delete את־נפש, for the sake of the metre.

| | | |
|---|---|---|
| 10 | I hear the talking of many: | |
| | 'Come, let us denounce him! | (5) |
| | All you who are friends to him, watch his steps! | (4) |
| | Perhaps he can be deceived, that we can overcome him | |
| | and take our revenge on him'. | (7) |
| 11 | But Yahweh is with me, as a dread warrior, | |
| | my persecutors will stumble, not overcome. | (4 + 4) |
| | They will be bitterly disappointed, that they are unsuccessful | |
| | with unforgettable shame. | (7) |
| 13 | Sing to Yahweh, praise Yahweh, | |
| | for he has delivered the poor man from the hand | |
| | of the evil man! | (4 + 4) |

The mood here is different from that in the preceding song (20.7-9).[65] The main concern there is that Jeremiah is being laughed at, scorned | [49] and ill-treated; here he is being lain in wait for and persecuted. Nor is Jeremiah's frame of mind the same: there, despair, here a stubborn determination to fight. We are thus dealing with two different songs,[66] which have been placed together on the basis of the arrangement of key-words—יכל and פתה.

The piece again begins abruptly, like the preceding one, without mention of the divine name. With horror he hears the secretive talk of 'many'; 'many' are uniting against him, the 'one'. The 'many' are often found in this sense in the psalms of lament (Pss. 3.3[1]; 4.7[6]; 31.14[13]; 55.19[18]; 56.3[2]; 119.157; cf. p. 25).

After the first sentence our text interjects a comment, 'terror on every side', which recurs in the book of Jeremiah in 6.25; 20.3f. 46.5; 49.29. The first of these passages reads:

Go not forth into the field, nor walk on the road;
For the enemy has a sword—terror on every side!

That cry very effectively sums up all the horrors of the vision. Text-critically it is beyond dispute. Cornill is right to reject Erbt's suggestion that גרה should be read in place of מגור; in any case the Greek translation need not be followed, since it never renders this expression precisely and never in the same way. The meaning of the expression is similar in 46.5 and 49.29, but those songs in all probability do not go back to Jeremiah.[67] The fourth passage, 20.3f., is a different matter. Cornill and Erbt have quite correctly contested Duhm's view that the narrative 19.1–20.6 is simply a midrash. When Pashkur releases Jeremiah from the stocks, the latter calls to him: 'Yahweh calls you not Pashkur, but Māgōr missābīb!', with the addition in vv. 4–6 bringing a longer self-contradictory explanation— or rather several of them. מסביב (v. 3) is missing in G and has apparently been added in assimilation to the other passages (Cornill, Erbt). Pashkur then is to be called Māgōr instead. To obtain a greater similarity in sound, Erbt instead suggests Māgūr, 'downfallen'. This seems not to be at all necessary, since G in any case renders the name as Pashkur throughout the book of Jeremiah. What the name Pashkur means, or how it could be interpreted is completely beside the point. For the word-play a general resemblance in sound was sufficient, without any connection in meaning. A corresponding word-play in German would be: not Arnold, | [50] but 'Unhold' ('fiend'). Such word-plays seem really banal to us; Hebrew tastes were different. This passage cannot therefore be called into consideration in order to explain that cry. We may, however, look to Ps. 31.14a[13a], which agrees word for word with Jer. 20.10α. But there is still a difference. In the psalm, that cry replaces the verbatim citation of the tittle-tattle, by expressing its effect; in Jeremiah, the content of the talk follows on from the cry, which in the present case can only be taken as an aside. Presumably it has been interpolated here from the psalm passage,[68] because there was agreement between the preceding sentences in the two places.

So they want to denounce Jeremiah[69] and therefore seek to incite him to say something with which they can catch him out. They reckon on the prophet being easily carried away by his passion and saying an ill-considered word against the temple or the king, which might cost him his head. That one's closest friends and relatives also join forces with the enemy (12.6) is often the subject of painful laments in the Psalms (Pss. 38.12[11]; 41.10[9] [איש שלומי]; 88.8, 19[8, 18]; Job 19.13-19),[70] and we often hear of evil plans and slanders there. But never of denunciation. How could they go so far as to report the poor invalid to the authorities on top of everything else! Things are quite different with the prophet, who recognized no political or priestly authority over him and thus frequently enough came into conflict with these powers (cf. Amos 7.10ff.; Jer. 26.7ff., 20ff.; 36; 38.1ff.).

The thought of being constantly watched is an awful one for the outspoken prophet. He himself knows how careless he is in the choice of his words and how easy it would be for them to tie a noose for him, even without actually falsifying his words. Powerless, he sees himself at the mercy of his enemies. But no: Yahweh is on his side! Yahweh, the fierce warrior! עריץ, 'violent', characterizes Jeremiah's mood. The very fact that in reference to Yahweh it almost sounds blasphemous[71] tells for its genuineness. Here, though, Jeremiah is not the mild, longsuffering character that we usually imagine him to be. He positively gloats over the thought of Yahweh falling upon his enemies | [51] and settling the score.

In terms of content, v. 11 is a 'trust-motif' which then changes into the 'assurance of being heard'. The vocabulary is drawn largely from the songs of lament. On רדפי cf. 15.15; 17.18 and the parallels cited there; on כשל, Ps. 9.3; on בוש and כלם, 17.18 and p. 27. The word השכיל is at home in the wisdom literature (Pss. 36.4[3]; 94.8; Prov. 10.5, 19; 14.35; 15.24; 16.20, 23; 17.2; 19.14; 21.12).

And now he even strikes up his thanksgiving song for his rescue (v. 13), as is often the case in the Psalms (see above, pp. 36f.). This verse is often deleted,[72] but hardly with justification. That its 'characteristically psalmic tone' cannot be admitted as an argument against authenticity should be evident from our whole discussion. Nor can much significance be attached to the fact that Jeremiah never actually escapes from persecution and shameful treatment (Duhm). For it is an *anticipatory* celebration, expressed in the midst of misery and distress, the fruit of hope and longing, and thus perfectly possible even for Jeremiah. And the most that the mention of 'the poor man' tells us is that there may already have existed at that time 'poor-man songs'[73] of the type we find in the Psalter.[74] After the prophets' complaints about social conditions, the prerequisites for such songs were doubtless given. Amos already presupposes the existence of the 'righteous poor' (2.6; 5.12). So too Jeremiah, with his way of applying the song-of-lament expressions to his own circumstances, could easily describe himself in this way. In the Psalms, too, there are occasional instances of the poet identifying himself at the end of the song, if not by name, at least by implication, in the mention of his status (Pss. 109.31; 18.51[50]).

The structure is once again that of the song of lament: v. 10, lament (opponents' plan); v. 11, trust-motif and assurance of being heard; v. 13, thanksgiving song. The aim to denounce, and probably also the phraseology in v. 11aα, point to a prophet being the author.

*Appendix*

# POEMS RELATED TO THE SONGS OF LAMENT

The following few poems are ones which do not conform so exactly to the songs of lament style but which are nonetheless related to them in content.

## 6. *12.1-6*

*Verse 1*, in this form, comprises a pentameter, a trimeter and a heptameter or double trimeter; to eliminate the trimeter as a gloss (Rothstein) is inadmissible, since it is indispensable in its content. By deleting the יהוה, Erbt obtains a heptameter for the first half of the verse, a, bα too, which is then immediately followed by the second heptameter. But to delete the divine name at the opening of the song is perilous. Cornill makes matters easier for himself by deleting the words כי אריב אליך, but these, too, are also difficult to do without; and in particular the objections based on content, which lead him to make the deletion, collapse in the light of our interpretation (see below). One would be better advised, if not content with the transmitted text, to read צִדְקַת (Giesebrecht) or תִּצְדַּק (Budde) in place of צדיק אתה. With Duhm and Erbt I read עליך and אתך. I see no reason to delete דרך and supply צלחו (Rothstein).

*Verse 2*. I would want to keep ילכו in spite of G (ילדו), since the imagery of the tree continues; as in Hos. 14.7 it simply means 'grow'.

*Verse 3*. ו תראני is missing in G and should be deleted as a variant for ידעתני (Hitzig). Verse 3bα is also missing in G (not in SV), but is indispensable in view of its parallelism to bβ and must have dropped out of the G text by some oversight (Duhm). התקם is suspicious: only the meaning 'tear off', 'cut off', is attested; in the usual translation, 'tear out', the essential information as to whether this is to be out of the sheep-fold or out of the flock, which is not self-evident, has to be supplied. Following Isa. 34.2 one could suggest הַחֲרִימֵם, which has a similar shape in the old Hebrew script. One is still more inclined to read תִּקָּחֵם, 'carry them off'; it is by no means rare for an imperfect (jussive) to stand in parallel to the imperative (Pss. 10.15; 17.8; 51.14, 20[13, 19]; 54.3[2]; 59.2[1]; 64.2[1]; 71.2; 142.2-5 [1-4]).

*Verse 4*. Duhm and Hölscher rightly reject the exclusion of this verse by Hitzig, Giesebrecht, Erbt, Cornill, Rothstein and H. Schmidt. Only bβ is to be deleted (Hölscher)—perhaps a fragment from a similar context; it seems to be a description of the ungodly (cf. Pss. 64.6[5]; 73.11; 94.7), which however contradicts the statement in v. 2bα and is surplus to the metre. For ועשב כל־השדה one is better advised to read וכל־עשב השדה with G and following Gen. 2.5; Exod. 9.22, 25 (10.12, 15) (BH). For בהמות read בְּהֵמָה (Rothstein).

*Verse 5*. כי should be deleted, with G; so too the article of סוסים (Cornill). For אתה בוטח I read לא תבטח following G^B, as Erbt already supposed; Hitzig's conjecture, אַתָּה בוֹרֵחַ, also adopted by Cornill, Duhm, Ehrlich and others, is thus unnecessary.

*Verse 6b* is rather overloaded, and at least the second גם־המה and בם (אליך also?) are to be deleted (cf. Erbt). When Jeremiah's relatives call after him at the top of their voices (מלא) he hears it too and has no need to be warned (v. 6bβ). Perhaps כְּלִמָּה should be read instead (Gunkel), which in Ezek. 34.29; 36.6f., 15, means 'reproach' (probably Ps. 89.51b[50b] should also be read this way; cf. Baethgen, Staerk, Kittel). For קרא with a direct object in the accusative cf. Jer. 3.12; 7.2; 2 Kgs 23.16. | [53]

| | | |
|---|---|---|
| 1. | Thou art in the right, Yahweh, when I argue with thee, | |
| | and yet I must take thee to task: | (7) |
| | Why is the way of the ungodly blessed, | |
| | and why do all live without care who act treacherously? | (7) |
| 2. | Thou hast planted them, and they take root, | |
| | they grow and bring forth fruit. | (3 + 3) |
| | Near art thou in their mouth | |
| | but far art thou in their heart! | (3 + 3) |
| 3. | But thou, Yahweh, knowest me, | |
| | triest my heart, how it stands toward thee— | (3 + 3) |
| | Carry them off like sheep to the slaughter | |
| | and set them apart for the day of throttling! | (3 + 3) |
| 4. | How long will the land yet mourn | |
| | and all the herbs of the field be withered? | (3 + 3) |
| | Before the wickedness of its inhabitants | |
| | beast and bird are swept away!— | (3 + 3) |
| 5. | 'You raced with men on foot and they wearied you— | |
| | how will you compete with horses? | (3 + 3) |
| | And in a safe land you are not confident— | |
| | how will you do in the jungle of Jordan? | (3 + 3) |
| 6. | Even your brothers and the house of your father, | |
| | even they have dealt treacherously with you, | (3 + 3) |
| | They call after you a reproach; | |
| | trust not, though they speak friendly words!' | (3 + 3) |

The problem with which Jeremiah is struggling here is the good fortune of the ungodly. The longstanding tenet that Yahweh makes things go well for the righteous and badly for the wicked seemed often to be contradicted by experience. Posterity then had to come to terms with this contradiction. The other 'Job-poetry' that we possess is generally presumed to belong to the post-exilic period (book of Job; Pss. 37; 49; 73; Mal. 2.17-3.5; Eccl. 8.14), so that one wonders whether the problem would already have existed in Jeremiah's time. But individualism in general seems really to have developed considerably at that time.[75] Ezekiel, in the eighteenth chapter of his book, deals in some detail with the idea of individual retribution, taking as his starting-point a traditional proverb that was in circulation at the time.[76] Such problems were thus known and experienced anew[77] at that period ||[54], so that a song like this should not seem strange on the lips of a man like Jeremiah, so long as there are no other objections to it. To understand the matter correctly one must always bear in mind that here Jeremiah is not speaking as a prophet but as an individual pious man who has difficulty with certain experiences he is having to face.

Since the good fortune of the wicked becomes a particularly painful problem when it is compounded by one's own misfortune, it is only natural that many of the forms and ideas proper to the songs of lament occur in the Job-poetry. So too here.

The very evenly structured poem immediately begins in a highly impassioned and embittered mood. צדיק here does not refer to the ethical quality (Cornill) but to the forensic: thou art in the right.[78] In bitter torment he stands up to his God and begins to remonstrate with him. The expression דבר משפטים את elsewhere refers to the activity of the judge (1.1b; 4.12; 39.5; 52.9), here Jeremiah uses it of himself—against Yahweh! This alone should prove that it is rather more than a 'calm, academic tone' that he uses in asking to be taught. Presumably he well knows that it is a hopeless enterprise to try to call Yahweh to account, that he will never get the better of him—and yet he cannot give up his attempt. It is rather like an oriental peasant reproaching the Kadi for his unjust and arbitrary decisions: even should it cost him his head, he must speak his mind (cf. Job 9.21; 12.13-15)!—The 'why' seems reminiscent of the song of lament, but there it is always למה, never מדוע as here.

The 'ungodly' are spoken of also in 5.26ff.; 23.19 (= 30.23); 25.31. In only the first of these passages is the authenticity undisputed; that of the others is strongly contested.[79] But in any case these passages yield nothing towards the understanding of the concept רשעים. In 5.26ff. they appear as people who have come to power and wealth by dubious means, which would be quite compatible with our passage. Things are going so well for them that one can only think that they stand under Yahweh's special protection. And yet it is only superficial reverence that they pay to Yahweh; deep down they are not concerned with him | [55] at all (v. 2). How different matters are with Jeremiah, Yahweh knows (v. 3a)![80] Other composers of 'Job-psalms' tend to say similar things (Ps. 73; Job 23.10-12; 31). The innocence motif of the songs of lament is comparable; with v. 3aα cf. Pss. 139.1-4; 142.4; with v. 3aβ cf. Pss. 17.3; 66.10; also Jer. 11.20 and the parallels cited there.[81] And since Yahweh finds nothing evil in Jeremiah Yahweh cannnot let him down either. Jumping thus from one idea to another—psychologically understandable—Jeremiah follows, as in 11.20, with the request for the annihilation of the ungodly. The same combination of these ideas, one's own innocence and the demand for punishment for the ungodly, is found in Ps. 139. 'Just piety cannot bear it when the ungodly are allowed to continue to exist' (Duhm). And the desire becomes even more understandable when the ungodly are at the same time tormenting and persecuting the pious. That this was the case with Jeremiah too is implied in v. 6.

In this request Cornill and Duhm see a contradiction of the expectation of the prophet found elsewhere: elsewhere he expects not a judgment against the wicked among the people but a catastrophe affecting them all. That is certainly so, but here Jeremiah is not speaking as a prophet, he is not proclaiming the word of Yahweh. Rather, here speaks the pious individual, who takes offence at the prosperity of the ungodly. It is thus not at all surprising that there should be a difference here with respect to his normal, 'prophetic' expectation.[82] Duhm's further objection, that Jeremiah otherwise never longs for disaster, is seen to be mistaken also. Here the concern is not with the people as a whole—though his heart bleeds when he has to announce their demise—but with those people whose doings go completely against his religious and moral sensitivities.

With v. 3, the petition has reached its climax. There follows an exclamation of impatience (v. 4), a further justification for v. 3b.[83] The whole land has been suffering, for so long, under this wickedness. The prophet is evidently looking back on a drought of several years' duration and on a great loss of cattle, and sees these phenomena as the effects of the curse that has been | [56] laid upon the land on account of the conduct of the wicked.

The notion that the land and its produce, often even its inhabitants, may be cursed by Yahweh on account of some wickedness, is frequently attested in the OT (cf. 4.27f.; 23.10; Hos. 4.3; Isa. 24.4-6; 33.9). That the notion does not belong only to a later period[84] is evident from the paradise story (Gen. 3.17ff.), from the story of the destruction of Sodom (Gen. 19) and from the curses due to the neglect of the laws (Deut. 28.15ff.; 29.18ff.; Lev. 26.14ff.). It makes little difference whether the whole population has participated in the wickedness or only a portion. Even the sin of an individual can result in a general punishment (Josh. 7). Thus, the 'sin of the inhabitants of Judea as a whole'[85] is not necessarily presupposed in v. 4. Jeremiah would like the punishment of the whole land to cease and the guilty to be punished instead. But does such a nationwide catastrophe not contradict the prosperity of the ungodly presupposed in vv. 1f.?[86] The apparent contradiction can, however, be explained (cf. Duhm) by taking the 'ungodly' of vv. 1f. as city capitalists, who are hardly affected by the drought and the loss of cattle. That a general calamity does not at all rule out the well-being of individuals is demonstrated by the present experience of these war years! Jeremiah is still well able to emphasize, on another occasion, how rich and poor suffer under the drought (14.2f.).

One has to assume a major paragraph division after v. 4, with which the prophet's passionate questioning and complaining ends. In vv. 5f. there follows, as the Targum has correctly recognized, Yahweh's answer. If one makes the prophet the speaker here as well (Ewald, Duhm), one obstructs from the outset the only way to understanding not only these verses but the whole song. Within our songs, again in 15.11f.[87] and 15.19ff. a divine speech follows the prophet's complaint, and in addition the position of 11.21-23 after 11.18-20 seems to have arisen because it was found to contain Yahweh's corresponding answer. It is true that in these cases the divine speech is always clearly introduced as such. But on the other hand there are enough divine words without any special introduction[88] for a similar omission not to be particularly surprising here. The divine speech falls into two parts: v. 5, two similitudes; v. 6, their application.

The *similitude* [*Gleichnis*], which serves to ensure the effect of a sentence by juxtaposing a similar sentence from another field, whose effect is not in doubt, must have been particularly attractive to the prophets | [57] with its vivid and graphic manner of speech, and was indeed used by them many times (cf. Isa. 1.3;[89] 10.15; 28.24ff.; Amos 3.3ff.; 5.19; 6.12). They are fond of placing together, as in this case, two similitudes that are similar in content; cf. Isa. 28.24ff. (various jobs and various tools); Amos 6.12 (running on rocks and ploughing the sea); *4 Ezra* 7.3ff. (sea and city). The similitude is always apt to present things in pairs; 'for the idea becomes clearer when I cast light on it from two sides'.[90] In both similitudes the observation moves from the smaller to the greater; we find the same *a minori ad maius* conclusion in *4 Ezra* 4.30f., in proverbial wisdom in Prov. 11.31; 19.10,[17] in the NT similitudes in Mt. 6.26ff.; 7.9ff.; 10.29ff.; Lk. 11.5ff.; 18.6ff.; Rom. 11.12. Finally a special refinement is the couching of the similitude in an interrogative form; so, 3.1aβ; 8.4; 13.23; 15.12; Amos 3.3ff.; 6.12; Isa. 10.15; Job 6.5f. The hearer—here and in 15.12 it is the prophet himself, in the other cases the people—is expected to answer the question for himself and then also apply it.[92]

The similitudes in our passage are saying: If you fail already on the easier task with the lesser danger, how will it be when it comes to the more difficult task and the greater danger? The following verse gives—as in Amos 6.12—the application of the similitude, which is often missing elsewhere in the prophets: even his nearest relatives will break faith with him—בגדו refers back to בגדי בגד in v. 1—and fall in with his enemies, so that in future he will stand in total isolation. This is the horse-race that faces him; this is the trek through the jungles along the Jordan where wild animals lie in wait! To understand this correctly we have to consider how close are the ties between the man of old and his family and what the break with them means for him.

The name-calling and ridiculing, the secret enmity hidden behind friendly words, we know from the Psalms. But the prophet too comes up against similar things. By reason of his separatist behaviour and his unshakable subscription to an ideal which the crowd find incomprehensible, he becomes the object of their scorn; by uncompromisingly trampling underfoot everything they hold sacred | [58] he draws their anger upon himself. Such is the lot of the prophet, and thus it was also Jeremiah's experience. To begin with he at least found some understanding and support among his relatives, or thought he did at any rate. But all at once it is as if scales fall from his eyes and he sees himself quite alone.

An answer to the question posed in v. 1 is thus not offered in vv. 5f. The deity refuses to account to him for the prosperity of the ungodly; Jeremiah is expected to continue to serve him even without an answer—to serve him *more*, in fact! Instead of responding to his question and comforting him, Yahweh promises that things will get worse; he must not be led astray by such rudimentary questions and doubts. How terrible for the prophet, and at the same time how humiliating! What he is complaining about now is not yet the worst; he was grumbling about the light burden, now he is to be given a heavy one. And so the problem that was his worry to date loses its significance; for this new experience is far more bitter! Though he is not spared the fact that even his nearest and dearest are בגדים he loses sight of the more distant בגדים. The greatness of the song lies in the way it leads on beyond the problem. Out of it speaks a resignation, a willingness to give up what has been dearest to him. With misunderstanding, enmity and persecution lying in wait all around him he is to continue on his way, quite alone—this is what Yahweh is showing him. And he accepts the burden; but no comforting thought weaves its way into his mind as we might have expected. Before him stands only the bitter fate that Yahweh has laid upon him.

Jeremiah has given expression to what he has been experiencing in these quiet and difficult hours, in a song whose form accommodates itself to that of the Job-psalms. But the insight that has finally come to him is for him dressed in the form of the divine speech, which gives him an answer to his bitter question and impetuous petition. Certainly, we will see a psychological explanation for this, in that this revelation, too, will come in actual fact from his own heart. But the prophet, for whom it is not at all unusual to hear God's voice, whose whole inner life, indeed, is split into two parts, human and divine, is firmly convinced that God is speaking to him here.[93]

Precisely because the ideas in question are so much opposed to his personal wishes, he must see them as something foreign to him, | [59] as something impressing itself upon him from outside.

We find similar conversations in *4 Ezra*, between Ezra and the angel, who there takes the place of God (4.1ff., 23ff., 33ff., 51ff.; 5.31ff.). His answers, too, are dismissive, though not so abrupt and severe as in Jeremiah's case; they are 'words which he would never have found in the light of his convictions as a man, quite different from what he would have wished for and expected and which deeply shock him'.[94] Exactly the same thing is true of Jeremiah.

It is here too that the peculiarity and greatness of our song lies, a song which in both form and content rises far above the level of the Psalms. The severity of the answer alone is sufficient to establish its authenticity; for all of the Job psalms the thought of the future demise of the ungodly is comfort enough. A song such as this can be expected only from a truly great man; and since it is ascribed to Jeremiah it will also derive from him.[95]

The structure of the song is as follows: v. 1a, introduction; vv. 1b, 2, question and reproach; v. 3a, innocence motif; v. 3b, request for vengeance; v. 4, complaint; vv. 5f., answer in the form of a divine speech. To some extent there are correspondences with the style of the song of lament. The reproachful question, which almost becomes an accusation, is characteristic of the Job poems (cf. Job 7.11ff.; 21.7ff.; 24.1ff.). And the strange introduction also points in this direction. Erbt (p. 173) sees in it the court-proceedings style; but this does not take adequate account of the peculiarity of the words. Certainly, expressions from court parlance are used (צדיק ,משפטים ,ריב דבר); but the peculiarity lies in the way they are used. Here it is God who is taken to court, as is often the case in Job (9.13-35; 13.3-22; 23.2-17).[96]

It remains for us to discuss the relationship of this song to 11.18-20, 21-23. In accordance with its place in the text, it has usually been seen as the immediate continuation of these verses.[97] But there can in any case | [60] be no question of a direct link, since at the very least there would have to be an intervening period during which Jeremiah waited in vain for the judgment announced in 11.22f. to come about. 12.1ff. gives no hint at all of a preceding promise or of any disappointment at its failure to be realized. Cornill instead wants to have 12.1ff. precede the other piece chronologically: 12.6 is the revelation spoken of in 11.18. But according to 11.18-23—for present purposes I take these verses as a unity, like Cornill—his persecutors are the people of Anathoth in general, there being no reason to include his own relatives at this point. Rather, that the latter persecute him too, clearly seems to be something new, an intensification of the general persecution.[98] If we go on to divide 11.18-23 into two pieces, then the second of these must, for the reason just given, come before 12.1-6. But with respect to the other piece, too, Cornill's assumption is scarcely probable. It would be strange if, just after Yahweh has informed him of the hostile conduct of his relatives, the prophet were promptly to point this out to him in such a passionate form as being something new.

The three pieces should thus be completely separated from one another, even though they have similar presuppositions. They can only gain from complete isolation; and if some things still remain unclear, this is due to the distinctive style and to a presentation that is not really intended for alien ears and eyes.

## 7. *15.10-12*

*Verse 10.* The second איש is not to be deleted, since the conclusion that G does not presuppose it (Rothstein) is questionable. Nor is לכל-הארץ superfluous or metrically exceptionable. The מ of מקללוני is to be taken with the previous word: כלהם קללוני(S).

*Verse 11* is so severely corrupt—in G even more, in parts, than in MT—that it can only be constructed very approximately. To go by MT it is undoubtedly a divine speech; the כה that is indispensable to אמר יהוה is found in G in v. 10b, where it has ended up as כחי (Giesebrecht). אם-לא also, which could at first sight also be understood differently, is well suited to a divine speech, since the latter often begins with such an asseveration (Num. 14.35; 2 Kgs 9.26; Isa. 5.9; 14.24; Jer. 22.6; Ezek. 5.11; 17.16, 19; 20.33; 34.8; 36.5; 38.19; Mal. 3.10). For שרותך I write אשרתיך (Gunkel); for לטוב in the sense of 'to a good outcome'; cf. Deut. 30.9b; Ps. 119.122 and לטובה. Verse 11b can then be understood as: I cause the enemy to intercede with you. This would be a promise, but a lame one, and it would preempt v. 12 inelegantly. The translations understand הפגעתי בך as 'to stand by someone'. In Isa. 64.4 (47.3?) also, פגע indicates an encounter in the good sense. This can thus be assumed for our passage too, without its being necessary to follow it by inserting the qal and the simple | [61] accusative. But in את-האיב there must be a mistake, both in MT and in the translations. I would tentatively suggest אתה אהבי; cf. Isa. 41.8.

*Verse 12.* ירע should be vocalized as a niphal. Here the song ends. *Verses 13f.* are in no way connected with it; they are identical with 17.3f., which is where they belong.

10.   Woe is me, Mother, that you bore me.
     the man of strife and contention for the whole land!   (3 + 3)
     I have not lent, nor have I borrowed,
     yet all of them curse me!   (5)
11.   Thus said Yahweh:
     'Truly, I lead you to the good,

> truly I stand by you; (3 + 3)
> In the time of trouble
> and in the time of distress—
> you are my friend! (6)
> 12. And does iron break,
> iron from the north, and bronze?' (5)[99]

The song begins[100] with a horrifying reproach against his own mother. Instead of being able to thank her for giving him life, he feels it would have been better if she had not done so. For what has become of him? He has become a man who lives in strife and contention with the whole world. And yet he has never lent money nor borrowed himself.

In the latter words Hölscher finds an emphasis that is strange in respect of Jeremiah, namely that he has not made any corrupt, usurious business deals. But the concern is not simply with lending but also with borrowing; it would be more correct to understand this as meaning that he has never been involved in everyday business deals, which so often give rise to strife and contention.[101] However, the sentence is not meant to be taken literally; it is a passionate metaphor: look, people treat me as if I were a wicked usurer or a tardy payer!

Since v. 10a does not contain an address to Yahweh, we are not dealing with a prayer and song of lament but—and this is indicated also by the passionateness of the words—with a Job-poem. The sequel, however (v. 10b), is unthinkable in that context and is only understandable on the lips of the prophet. When the prophet rejects the sacrificial cult and the dissolute life of the priests, and castigates the deceit of the false | [62] prophets, when he uncompromisingly unmasks social unjustices and pillories the prosperity of the rich, when he points out the sins of the royal household and condemns the politics being practised, when he announces the fall of the city, the destruction of the temple and the deportation of the people, then he arouses not only the opposition of the upper classes and the government but of the broad mass of the people, who see the men they are accustomed to looking up to with respect, slandered, and whose own most sacred patriotic and religious feelings are hurt. So he has everyone against him, nowhere finds a sympathetic response, and everywhere encounters the most vigorous opposition. Strong characters, such as an Amos or an Isaiah, very conscious of their divine commission, could take all this in their stride. A Jeremiah is not hard enough for this. His tender heart languishes under the incessant struggle and he longs for peace and quiet.

In vv. 11f. there follows an oracle which promises him Yahweh's support. Verse 11 needs no explanation; but v. 12 sounds cryptic and is quite a headache to exegetes.[102] But if v. 11 has been recognized to be a divine speech, in which case its mysteriousness would of course be quite fitting, we find an explanation for v. 12, suggested already by older exegetes,[103] which connects it with what has gone before. Iron obtained at the Pontus was famous far and wide in antiquity and would certainly have reached Palestine in trading.[104] This is what our verse alludes to. Though elsewhere the 'North' has a special meaning for Jeremiah, as the geographical direction from which he expects the enemy to come, this does not preclude his use of the word also in the quite usual sense, speaking here for example of 'northern iron'. As little as bronze and iron break, so little will you break; this is the idea.[105] The prophet is to stand up to the people like a brazen wall (1.18; 15.20). As is the way of the prophet, however, this is said in a veiled form. Again, as in 12.5, it is a similitude in interrogative form. Jeremiah has to provide the answer to the question for himself. The similitude, too,—unlike 12.5f.—is intentionally left without an interpretation; thus it really is mysterious and therefore genuinely prophetic. It should not be assumed that there was originally a conclusion following v. 12 which has now been lost; | [63] the effect would only be lessened by this.

Yahweh's answer thus does not promise him the peace that he longs for. Peace is not for the prophet. To be a prophet means to be a fighter—his many sorrows have brought him to this insight. But now he has the assurance that Yahweh is with him, so that he cannot succumb to his foes. And in this confidence he continues on his way.

The verses thus join together into a well-rounded whole: cry of lament with divine reply. In both parts the concern with the prophet is evident. Characteristics of the song-of-lament style are not present; the mood is primarily that of the Job poems, but transcends these in the oracle.

## 8. *20.7-9*

*Verse 7.* I read החזקתני (Ehrlich).

*Verse 8.* כל־היום is an appendage and is to be deleted as a gloss on v. 7 (Erbt).

*Verse 8*. It is unnecessary to emend דבר יהוה to דברך (Rothstein); v. 9 also speaks of Yahweh in the third person: the prophet has so to speak turned away from Yahweh and carries on talking to himself. If one goes as far as to read דברי (Duhm), the whole point is lost.

*Verse 9*. Perhaps ואם אמרתי should be read (Ehrlich); cf. Ps. 94.18; Job 9.27. בלבי is missing in G but may still be genuine. It is better not to emend עצר into כצרב 'like inflammation' (Duhm, Ehrlich); עצר is not grammatically impossible (Gesenius-Kautzsch, §132d), and inflamation would not be a very appropriate metaphor for the fire that is straining to get out. It is unnecessary to insert שאת or לשאת after אוכל (Cornill, Duhm, BH) in accordance with G; אוכל used absolutely is more effective (cf. Isa. 29.11). Verse 9c may on no account be deleted as 'dispensable' (against Rothstein).

| | | |
|---|---|---|
| 7. | Thou didst lead me astray, Yahweh, and I let myself be led astray; | |
| | thou didst set about me and hast prevailed. | (5) |
| | I have become a laughingstock all the time, everyone mocks me. | (5) |
| 8. | For whenever I speak, I cry out for help, I shout, 'Violence and oppression!' | (3 + 3) |
| | For the word of Yahweh became for me shame and derision. | (5) |
| 9. | And if I think I will not remember him or speak any more in his name, | (3 + 3) |
| | Then there is in my heart as it were a burning fire, shut up in my bones. | (6) |
| | I struggle to bear it and cannot. | (4) |

The poem, which despite its brevity is so full of meaning, begins with a bitter, passionate reproach: 'Thou didst lead me astray!' The verb here | [64] (פתה) really means 'to talk someone into something', and is the usual term for the seduction of a maiden (Exod. 22.15[16]; Sir. 42.10; cf. Hos. 2.16[14]). The metaphor, which is only a weak allusion, is immediately followed by another, taken from wrestling. Using these bold, but incomparably vivid images, the prophet depicts how he has, half willingly, half under coercion, placed himself in Yahweh's service: 'How sweet wast Thou to me, and how strong!' But now, like a girl left stranded in shame, full of bitterness he must lament: 'Oh, if only I had not let myself be led astray!' For now he reaps nothing but scorn and derision.

Though v. 7a undoubtedly bears the mark of the prophet (for where would the psalmist be who would know how to tell of such experiences?), v. 7b would be equally at home in the Psalms (cf. Pss. 22.8[7]; 44.14; 69.12; 79.4; 109.25). The fate of the prophet and that of the psalmist coincide in the fact that they both have to suffer mockery and persecution.[106] Though the cause is not the same, the result certainly is. Verse 8a, too, can apply to a psalmist as well as to the prophet. זעק is a standing expression in the lament of the Psalms;[107] for חמס see Pss. 27.12; 35.11; 55.10[9]; 140.2, 5, 12[1, 4, 11]; Job 19.7. שׁד, however, is found there only at Ps. 12 and twice each in Job and Proverbs, while it is common in the Prophets, thus clearly belonging to the preferred speech of the prophets.

Every time Jeremiah opens his mouth, it is to shout about the violence to which he is being subjected. He can no longer speak otherwise! What an unbearable fate for such a man, to have to endure such constant abuse (cf. Isa. 50.6)! Verse 8b explains why this has come upon him: it is because he is Yahweh's messenger and must proclaim Yahweh's word, he tells himself bitterly. As the envoy of the most high King he would surely have every right to be accepted with honour and be listened to attentively; but he is derided and slandered, and God's word becomes a mockery and a scandal!

Despite all the reminiscences of the Psalms style, v. 8 viewed as a whole should thus be taken as prophetic. In 6.10b also, Jeremiah complains that Yahweh's word has become an object of ridicule.

This tends often to spoil his whole prophetic office for him (v. 9). He would love to cast it at Yahweh's feet, not bother about Yahweh any more and be able to enjoy life, which in present circumstances is impossible for him (cf. 15.17). אמרתי, in the psalms of lament also, and in their various component parts in fact, serves to introduce an idea or a word[108] (Pss. 30.7[6]; |[65] 31.15, 23[15, 22]; 32.5; 38.17[16]; 39.2[1]; 94.18; 116.11; 119.57; 140.7[6]; 142.6[5]; Isa. 38.10f.).

In parallel with זכר[109] is the more precise דבר בשם. According to Hölscher, the ב was used merely to introduce the object of the verb to speak: 'I will no longer name his Name'[110]—as for example in דבר גאות (Ps. 17.10; cf. Ps. 73.8; Isa. 63.1; Dan. 9.21). However, when linked with שם it never means anything other than to speak in someone's name (1 Sam. 25.9). And this expression is used above all by the prophet, who speaks in Yahweh's name (26.16; 29.23; 44.16; Exod. 5.23; Deut. 18.19, 20, 22; 1 Kgs 22.16; Zech. 13.3; Dan. 9.6; 1 Chron. 21.19; 2 Chron. 18.15; 33.18); it is completely synonymous with the נבא בשם (התנבא) (11.21; 14.15; 23.25; 26.9, 20; 27.15; 29.9,

21) with which it is interchangeable in the same context.

But the prophet's attempt to go his own way is not successful. The word of God that he wants to keep quiet burns like fire in his bones—בעצמותי,[111] also found in Ps. 42.11[10]; Lam. 1.13—and cannot be suppressed for long. It has to be proclaimed, no matter how terrible the consequences will be for him. He can suppress the expression of the thoughts, but not the thoughts themselves! On the contrary, the less he speaks about it, the hotter the inner fire becomes, until finally it pours out again in words after all. Two passages in the songs of lament sound similar: in Ps. 32.3f. the psalmist cannot suppress his confession of sin, in Ps. 39.3f.[2f.] his pain. Though these are experiences which any pious person might have, the content of our passage only fits the prophet, who stands under an obligation and has to prophesy (4.19a; Amos 3.8; 1 Cor. 9.16).[112] And so he makes his appearance again as a prophet—he can do no other. But the fate laid upon him is hard to bear—the song thus ends without a comforting prospect of any kind.

The echoes of the songs of lament style are not as strong here as in the earlier songs. Where such elements are present, they belong to the lament. The ideas in vv. 7a and 9a are prophetic, even if outwardly v. 9a also has certain parallels in the Psalter. | [66] Taken as a whole, too, the song assumes a position of its own; it contains a coherent narrative about the author's own person, such as we really only find in the thanksgiving song (eg. Pss. 18.5ff., 17ff.[4ff., 16ff.]; 30.3f., 7ff.[2f., 6ff.]; 34.5ff.[4ff.]; Isa. 38.10ff.; Jon. 2.3ff.) and in the didactic poem (e.g. Pss. 32.3ff.; 73.13ff.).[113] But even if the kind of narrative it is perhaps derives from this source, that will not be the case for its individual parts. From a literary-critical point of view, therefore, this song constitutes a completely independent entity.

### 9. *20.14-18*

*Verse 14.* Both instances of אשר are to be deleted.

*Verse 15.* אשר and לאמר are to be deleted.

*Verse 16.* האיש ההוא is an explicative that has been added secondarily (Duhm). To cancel עת in accordance with G (Duhm) seems inappropriate to me in view of the metre.

*Verse 17.* Since the meaning 'still in the womb' cannot be demonstrated for מֵרחם, it will be a miswriting of בְרחם, due to the influence of the following words (Cornill, Duhm, Erbt).

14.  Cursed be the day, on which I was born;
     the day on which my mother bore me, be without blessing. (4 + 4)
15.  Cursed be the man who brought the news to my father:
     'A son is born to you!'—making him very glad.     (4 + 4)
16.  Let him be like the cities
     which Yahweh overthrew without pity.     (6)
     Let him hear a cry of woe in the morning
     and a war-cry at noon!     (3 + 3)
17.  Because he did not kill me in the womb     (3)
     so that my mother was my grave
     and her womb for ever great     (3 + 3)
18.  Why did I come forth from the womb—
     to see toil and sorrow,
     that my days should be spent in shame?     (3 + 3)[114]

Once again we see the prophet in a state of intense despair. He execrates his life, his birth (cf. 15.10). The only bit of restraint shown is the fact that he at least spares his own parents. The prophet broods over his existence, which is devoid of all joy and honour. In bitter pain, in impotent anger at this pitiful fate, he curses the day of his | [67] birth, which of course everyone else regards as a happy day; in fact he even curses the man who brought his father the good news that he had a son—and not a daughter! Full of bitterness, he now thinks: how unfounded his joy was! And then, after a pause, perhaps,—the metre also changes at v. 16—he returns to that day and showers it with new curses. It would have been better to have died in the womb than to have been born for such a wretched existence.[115] There is no indication of the particular cause for this painful outburst, and the cause can only be surmised by analogy with the other songs.[116]

In its form this song differs substantially from the poems of lament. It is not directed to Yahweh and is therefore not a prayer. One might call it a *self-curse*. Some of the individual expressions in v. 18 are reminiscent of the songs of lament: so למה (see above, p. 27), עמל (Pss. 10.14; 25.18; 55.11[10]; 90.10), יגון (Pss. 13.3[2]; 31.11[10]; 116.3); for v. 18b compare Ps. 31.11[10] and 102.4[3]. Markedly prophetic ideas or expressions are not to be found. There is, however, a connection with the other songs in that there is some correspondence in mood.

We have a counterpart to this song in Job 3, a poem that has striking points of contact with our poem, but is very much longer.

The song in Jeremiah, in its simple, brief form, makes a far deeper impression than that one, which is more artistic and more deliberate, but also somewhat overloaded and cold (Duhm). It is thus correct that the dependence is generally seen to lie with Job.[117]

Chapter 4

# THE RELATION OF JEREMIAH'S POEMS OF LAMENT
# TO THE SONGS OF LAMENT TYPE

## 1. *The Authenticity of the Poems of Lament in Jeremiah*

Stade, N. Schmidt and Hölscher felt their demonstration of the psalm-like character of our songs was sufficient justification for deleting them as inauthentic. We must now try to discover what kind of considerations actually led them to this conclusion.

First of all is the perfectly correct recognition of the real differences in personality between the psalmist and the prophet. Over the last decades, the better our comprehension of the nature of prophecy has become, the greater the distance between it and the psalms literature has necessarily appeared. Whereas in the middle of the last century many psalms were being unashamedly derived from prophets, today the practice has been almost completely abandoned. Now, not only as regards their piety and poetic method but in their whole nature, we are struck by only the great difference between them.

Furthermore, it had been recognized that later Judaism loved to insert psalms into the Old Testament books. Songs that in no way differed from those in the Psalter were found scattered not only in the historical books but equally so in the prophetic ones. And finally there was the view, rapidly gaining ground, that psalms composition did not come into being at all until about the time of the exile.[1]

The 'inauthentic' verdict will have been based on considerations such as these. But can one agree with them at all?

The question of the age of psalms composition will be discussed later. This difference between the nature of the prophet and that of the psalmist | [69] cannot be denied, nor indeed the difference in poetic methods. But the fact remains that the prophets took over poetic forms that were inherently foreign to them, making them their own. This was demonstrated more than thirty years ago with reference to the dirge.[2] Today we know the same is true of a whole range of both cultic and secular song types.[3] And so not every psalm-type song in a prophetic book must necessarily be a later addition; rather, it depends completely on the type of the song and the nature of the prophet. We would more readily ascribe a song of lament to a Jeremiah—indeed Hölscher speaks of the 'lyrical and sensitive tone of his poetic compositions' (p. 269)—than we would to an Isaiah, who does, however, occasionally make use of the dirge (1.21ff.). The possibility that Jeremiah composed such songs should not, therefore, be dismissed out of hand. And if, moreover, it can be demonstrated that on the one hand the psalms of the book of Jeremiah differ from those of the Psalter in characteristic ways, and in addition that these characteristics are associated with the prophetic manner, and if on the other hand similar lyrical sections are to be found in the genuine parts of the book of Jeremiah, then we should have positive proof of their authenticity.

a. Our third chapter attempted to determine for each individual song what features correspond to the style of the Psalms and which do not. Alongside the extensive agreement in structure and use of language that we discerned between Jeremiah's songs and the psalms of lament, a range of differences in form and content was also evident. We shall now draw these together, beginning with the *deviations from the songs of lament style*.

Some of these do not commence with the invocation, i.e. a formal address of the deity, but in the direct manner proper to prophetic speech (18.18: 20.10).[4] The place of the assurance of being heard, which occurs only at 20.11, is often taken by a divine speech (12.5f.; 15.11f., 19-21. 11.21-23 too, originally an independent piece, is now apparently viewed as an answer to 11.18-20). This is a very rare occurrence in the psalms of lament, where it is probably due to the influence of prophetic style,[5] but it is quite understandable in the case of the prophet, who is so at home with the form | [70] of the divine speech. Only the prophet, not the psalmist, really leads such a double life. While the psalms style on the whole makes only limited use of concrete terms, in particular avoiding the naming of names, here Jeremiah is mentioned by name (18.18; cf. also the naming of Anathoth in 11.21, 23). Besides the למה of the song of lament, which asks after the purpose (15.18; 20.18), we also find מדוע (12.1), which asks after the cause.

More numerous and even more significant are cases in which the ideas expressed show evidence of prophetic substance. The author of these songs receives special knowledge from Yahweh (11.18). Yahweh's name is named over him (15.16) and it is in Yahweh's name that he speaks (20.9). He is to stand before Yahweh as his servant (15.19; 18.20) and be his mouthpiece (15.19). He is reproached that Yahweh's word has not been fulfilled (17.15), and he insists that he has not desired the catastrophe to come about (17.16) but rather interceded for the people (18.20). Yahweh's hand comes upon him (15.17) and Yahweh fills him with his anger (15.17). To the people he is to stand like a bronze wall (15.20), but his enemies want to provoke him into making ill-considered statements so that they can bring a charge against him (20.10). In fact, song-of-lament motifs are filled with prophetic content:[6] the protestation of innocence (17.16) and the speech of the ungodly (17.15) are given a specifically prophetic colouring, and the innocence motif can even become a prophetic lament (15.17).

Consequently a prophetic origin is established beyond all doubt for no fewer than nine of our ten songs. Only in 20.14-18 is no prophetic characteristic to be found.[7] However, it is not difficult to relate 20.18 to the awful experiences encountered in his prophetic ministry, and the mood of despair prevalent here also appears there occasionally (15.10), so that the inner connection between this song and the others cannot be missed.

The peculiar mixture of the songs of lament style and the Job-poems with prophetic elements is thus the link between these songs—as long as they are not purely prophetic (11.21-23; 15.10-12)—just as they are also close in content, in their world of ideas. Not that they agree in all details. Among them there are those which conclude without a bright prospect of any kind (20.7-9, 14-18), those which look to the future seriously but resolutely (12.1-6; 15.10-12, 15-21), while others fade into an entreaty (17.14-18; 18.18-23), and in one the prophet soars to a peak of certainty | [71] and joyfully strikes up the thanksgiving song (20.10-13). Nor is the concern of the lament, i.e. the suffering that he is sighing over, always quite the same. But these are not contradictions that would cast doubt on the unity of authorship. In relation to the agreement in form and main content they are not substantial. They merely reflect a rich inner life that knows both courage and faintheartedness, both high points and low points.

In the mixture of which we spoke the prophetic element at first seems very much to take second place. On the whole these songs, in their structure and vocabulary, are psalms. Only on closer scrutiny does one come up against the prophetic features. However, though in form these are only secondary, their content means that their significance is considerably enhanced. They are all-important for an understanding of the songs; it is only when they are taken into account that one can appreciate the import and the value of the songs. Only then are they filled with real life for us. The reason for this is best seen when we compare them with those psalms in the Psalter which betray prophetic influence. We think of psalms which also show a mixed character, in that they have taken over, for example, the future expectation of prophecy—the 'eschatological hymns' (Pss. 46; 47; 48; 76; 93; 96; 97; 98; 99)—or follow the prophetic example and reject sacrifice (Pss. 40; 50; 51; 69). It is immediately evident what distinguishes them from the psalms of Jeremiah. In the former, *prophetic ideas and forms* have been adopted; in the latter, *prophetic experience* underlies the psalmic form. In the former case, the authors are psalmists who have learnt a lot from the prophets; here we have a prophet who clothes his most personal experiences in psalmic form.

b. The prophetic features of the psalms of Jeremiah show quite conclusively that they derive from a prophet. That Jeremiah is the author is thus already within the realm of possibility. And this possibility turns into probability when there are demonstrable points of agreement between them and the parts of the book of Jeremiah whose authenticity is acknowledged—agreement in content, but more particularly in form. The peculiarity of those songs lies in the way they combine the lyrical, the songs of lament style, with the prophetic. If we can show traces of this combination elsewhere in Jeremiah there should be no further objections whatsoever to the authenticity of those songs.

In our search for agreements in content, right at the outset we must reckon only with a small yield. In the other sections | [72] of the book of Jeremiah, the prophet is concerned with the people and its sin, with the king and political events, matters which cannot come to the fore in our songs, where the prophet is occupied with his own person and his own well-being. There the prophet appears in his external role, his 'professional' side; what we see here is the man and his struggle to come to terms with his prophetic role. There we see the prophet from the outside, here from the inside. And so the texts on each side must necessarily pass each other by. There may be contact between them at some points, but they can never coincide.[8]

And where we do find points of contact, they are usually of such a general nature that they are not much use. For the most part they are things which are not characteristic of Jeremiah but which he shares with all prophets. Of such a kind is the expectation of a coming catastrophe (17.16), which, however, is here sometimes seen as restricted to his enemies and persecutors; or the fact that Jeremiah really did often intercede on behalf of the people, which the songs also assume (18.20; cf. pp. 58f.). Individual linguistic correspondences are not much help either, e.g. the fact that the verbal form תתחרה (12.5) recurs only in 22.15. And if support for the Jeremianic character of the expression שנת פקדתם (11.23) is thought to be provided by 23.12; 8.12; 6.15, it is found more frequently in the inauthentic parts of the book (10.15; 46.21; 48.44; 50.27; 51.18).

It is of much greater importance that we find certain echoes of the songs of lament style also in sections of Jeremiah that are acknowledged to be genuine. I cite the relevant passages in the order in which they occur in the text.

| 4.19 | O my breast, my breast! I am quaking! | |
|---|---|---|
| | You chambers of the heart! | (5) |
| | My soul rages within me,[9] | (5) |
| | I cannot be silent | |
| | For I hear the sound of the horn, | |
| | the noise of war. | (5) |
| 20 | Disaster follows hard upon disaster; | |
| | for the whole land is laid waste, | (5) |
| | Suddenly my tents are destroyed, | |
| | my covers in a moment. | (5) |
| 21 | How long must I see the standard | |
| | and hear the sound of the horn? | (5) |

|[73] The song clearly begins with a lament; for v. 19aα cf. Pss. 55.5[4]; 38.11[10]; 39.4[3]. But the fact that he cannot be silent already points to the prophetic sphere (cf. 20.9; pp. 75f.). And the things that torment him, which he complains of, are the terrible visions and auditions that constantly pursue him and cannot be silenced. In v. 21 the lament again has a say. The phrase עד־מתי, taken from the song of lament, introduces the question, which can only, however, be

understood in the context of prophetic experience.

| 8.18 | Without healing,[10] grief weighs upon me.[11] | |
| | my heart is sick in me. | (5) |
| 19 | Yes, loud crying of my people | |
| | from the length and breadth of the land: | (5) |
| | 'Is Yahweh not in Zion, | |
| | is her king not there?'— | (5) |
| | 'Why did they provoke me with the idols, | |
| | illusions from foreign lands?'— | (5) |
| 20 | [12]'Past the summer, ended the autumn, | |
| | and no help for us!' | (5) |
| 21 | On account of the fall of my people I am in mourning,[13] | |
| | horror grips me. | (5) |
| 22 | Is there no balm in Gilead, | |
| | and is no physician there? | (5) |
| | [14]Why does not healing arise | |
| | for the daughter, my people? | (5) |
| 23 | O that my head were water, | |
| | my eye a fountain of tears | (5) |
| | That I might weep day and night | |
| | for the slain of my people! | (5) |

This poem, too, begins with a lament (for יגון cf. 20.18; Pss. 13.3[2]; 31.11[10]; 116.3) concerning the visions that pursue him. He can already hear the people's lament (v. 19aβ) and Yahweh's reproachful answer (v. 19b). Another picture then follows: once again lament of the people (v. 20), whereupon the prophet takes up his own lament (vv. 21-23), a question with מדוע and an exclamation that is again reminiscent of the song of lament (Pss. 6.7f.[6f.]; 31.10[9]; 42.4[3]), but has a prophetic colouring.

|[74] The song of 10.19-22 has a similar beginning, too:

> Woe is me because of my wound, [15]incurable is my blow!
> Yes, this is my pain,[16] which I must bear![17]

The words שבר, מכה and חלי originally refer to physical suffering and are borrowed from the song of lament; cf. 15.18; 17.14. Here, too, the cause of his pain is the vision of the imminent disaster which the following verses describe.

The short song of 13.17 also belongs here.

| [17]My soul weeps in quiet | |
| over the pride.[18] | (5) |

> My eye flows with tears
> > that Yahweh's flock is taken captive.     (5)

The prophet weeps in secret—this should not of course be interpreted in accordance with 36.19, with Duhm and Cornill (p. 180), rather he must not show weakness in front of the people—because in his mind he sees the people already carried off. The phraseology is reminiscent of 8.23.

In 14.17f. he gives an even more graphic description of the horrors of a vision:

| 17 | My eyes flow with tears, | |
| | Day and night, without end. | (7) |
| | For terribly smitten is the daughter,[19] my people, | |
| | incurable indeed is her wound.[20] | (7) |
| 18 | If I go out into the field— | |
| | behold those slain by the sword! | (5) |
| | If I go into the city— | |
| | behold those tormented by hunger.[21] | (5) |

The wording of the lament is similar to 8.23 and 10.19. 23.9 marks the conclusion of this series:

> My heart is broken in my body,
> > all my bones are shaking.     (3 + 3)
> I am like a drunken man,
> > like one whom wine has confused,[22]     (3 + 3)
> |[75] Before Yahweh
> > and before his holy words.[23]     (5)

Here Jeremiah describes the effect of a vision with terms drawn in part from the song of lament; the first half-line recalls 4.19 and the parallels mentioned there, the second recalls passages such as Pss. 6.3[2]; 22.15[14]; 31.11[10]; 32.3; Lam. 3.4, while the imagery in the second line is original.

Baruch's lament should also be mentioned in this context.

> Woe is me, for Yahweh heaps
> > sorrow upon my pain.     (3 + 3)
> I am weary with sighing
> > but I find no rest (45.3)     (5)

Duhm was the first to recognize a poem here. Cornill pointed out the generality and indefiniteness of the words—what the situation is can thus only be roughly surmised—which is explicable in that the song of lament style has been used.[24] For יגון refer to 8.18 and 20.18, for מכאב to Pss. 38.18[17] and 69.27[26], for v. bα to Ps. 6.7[6] (for יגע cf. also Ps. 69.4[3], for אנחה Pss. 31.11[10]; 38.10[9] and 102.6[5] ). The lament is followed by Yahweh's reply via Jeremiah (45.4f.), in a similar fashion for 12.1-6; 15.10-12, 15-21. As in these cases, the reply signals a refusal of the petition.

12.7-13 is a song of a different type again. The peculiar character of this song, first recognized by Erbt (p. 262), has also been correctly perceived by Hölscher (p. 296). It is a lament by Yahweh, which gradually turns into a threat. It really employs only the mood of the lament, it is true; expressions peculiar to the song of lament are not used.

It is virtually unanimously accepted that the songs mentioned derive from Jeremiah. Hölscher, too (pp. 399f.), counts them among the certainly genuine components of the book.[25] Only N. Schmidt deletes 4.19-21; 8.18-21; 10.17-25; 12.7-13; 13.15-17 as poetic additions.[26] But, though he thereby proves to be somewhat more consistent than Hölscher, he has himself overlooked a number of other such echoes of the psalms (11.18-20, 21-23; 14.17; 45.3). But nobody is going to feel tempted to make up for this | [76] and dispense with all of these songs. It was with good reason that Hölscher restricted his denial of authenticity to precisely these songs. He certainly perceived the lyrical force of this and many other passages, but alongside it the prophetic base too. In many cases it is only the beginning that is lyrical, and sometimes perhaps the end of the song. The remainder is prophetic and determines the overall impression. And this is what makes for the difference between these songs and the 'psalms' of Jeremiah. In both, prophetic and lyrical elements are combined; but the kind of combination varies. In one case—if we can express the relationship in a literary formula—we have *psalms with prophetic elements*, while in the other we have *prophetic songs with echoes of the psalms*. And between the two are the pieces discussed in the appendix above (pp. 63ff.), in which the lyrical aspect is less pronounced than in the first group, but more pronounced than in the second. The important point is that the lyrical element is also found in passages in Jeremiah whose authenticity is not doubted, so that there is a bridge stretching from these to the 'psalms of Jeremiah'. If it is incontestable that Jeremiah occasionally adopts a lyrical tone, the possibility must also be admitted that he makes use of thoroughly lyrical types in other places too.

And this is more than just a formal correspondence. What makes the psalms of Jeremiah so distinctive is, in the final analysis, rooted in Jeremiah's personality itself.

For Jeremiah differs from his predecessors primarily in the position he adopts towards his God and the prophetic ministry. Men such as Amos, Hosea, Isaiah and Micah give themselves unreservedly to their prophetic 'profession' and are devoted to it. They gladly submit to the compulsion they are under, even through all the personal sacrifices and sufferings that it may bring them. Jeremiah, on the other hand, only obeys the prophetic impulse under protest and only out of necessity. A good indication of this lies in the difference between his call and that of Isaiah. While Isaiah responds to Yahweh's query as to whom he should send by immediately offering himself (6.8), Jeremiah shrinks back at the immensity and difficulty of the task imposed upon him; he tries to withdraw from it and has first to be encouraged by Yahweh and assured of Yahweh's support (1.6ff.). At other moments, too, there is often evidence of a degree of resistance. He cannot just be a prophet; purely human needs and feelings put in their own claims. He finds it painful that he, who sees before him the terrible calamity of his people, should be denied a woman's love and | [77] family bliss, that he should be excluded from all human joy and happiness, and that he should become more and more isolated (16.1ff.). He finds it hard, too, to come to terms with the fact that his life's work among the people produces so little success and that all he has to announce to them is disaster and punishment (5.1ff.; 9.1ff.). This is why his proclamation of doom is so often vibrant with a peculiarly personal tone (4.23ff.; 5.4; 9.1[27]); here, as in the summons to the dirge (6.26), we sense the pain that he experiences on account of his gloomy message. He feels far more sorry for the people than Amos (7.1-9; 8.1ff.) and Isaiah (6.11), and Yahweh has constantly to reject his intercession for them (7.16; 11.14; 14.11; 15.1; 27.18). It is, in fact, striking how often in the book of Jeremiah—even if we do not count the actual visions—Yahweh speaks to his prophet (3.6ff., 11ff.; 6.27ff.; 7.16ff.; 11.9ff.; 14.11ff.; 16.1ff.; 18.1ff.); occasionally this even develops into a dialogue between them (14.11-16). This is connected with Jeremiah's inner struggles, which necessitate special coaxing and persuasion on Yahweh's part. A deep crack thus runs through Jeremiah's personality. His Ego is to a certain extent split; at least for periods of time, the human being and the prophet in him part company.

But this picture, which is drawn from the parts of the book that are acknowledged to be authentic, is fully confirmed in the 'poems of lament', in which the same double life is expressed. The resistance of the human being in him to the burden of the prophetic office, the pronounced dialogue form, the reply of the deity to his complaints and accusations, have here found their most poignant expression.

c. The findings we have gathered are reinforced further by the recognition that the literary type most closely related to the individual song of lament, namely the *communal song of lament*,[28] is also well represented in Jeremiah.

Two of these are to be found in ch. 14.[29] The first comprises 14.2-10—the superscript of v. 1 does not fit with the following verse, where to begin with Yahweh does not speak at all—in which the following components may be discerned: vv. 2-6, lament, description of calamity (drought) (cf. Pss. 44.10ff.[9ff.]; 74.1ff.; 79.1ff.); v. 7, repentance motif (cf. Ps. 90.8); v. 8a, renewed invocation (for מקוה ישראל cf. 17.13; | [78] for מושיעו Pss. 7.11[10]; 17.7[6]); vv. 8b, 9a, new lament with the familiar 'why' (cf. Pss. 10.1, 13; 44.24f.[23f.]; 74.1, 11; 80.13[12]); v. 9b, trust motif with a negatively expressed petition (cf. Pss. 10.12; 44.24[23]; 74.19); v. 10, the divine reply, which rejects the petition.[30] The authenticity of the song is generally accepted, even by Hölscher (p. 399).

The other song comprises 14.19–15.2: v. 19, lament in the form of a question (for 'reproach', cf. Ps. 44.10[9], 60.3, 12[1, 10]; 74.1; thereafter a 'why' again, as in 14.1, though here it is מדוע); v. 20, repentance motif (guilt of the fathers also in Lam. 5.7); v. 21, petition, which attempts to appeal to Yahweh's honour (cf. Pss. 79.9, 12; 94.5; for זכר cf. Pss. 74.18; 89.48, 51[47, 50]; for the reminder of the covenant, Pss. 44.18[17]; 74.20; 89.40[39]); v. 22 praises in hymnic tones Yahweh's superiority over the gods of the heathen, at the same time revealing the outward occasion of the song, a drought. In 15.1f., Yahweh's reply follows, negative and devastating, as in 14.10. The authenticity of this piece is heavily disputed, it is true,[31] though the grounds for such a view are not exactly compelling.

In the case of the third song, however, we are again on firm ground as far as authenticity is concerned. The song stands within a larger liturgical context (3.21–4.4). 3.21 describes the calamity and the general lamenting, in v. 22a Yahweh calls the people to repentance, promising them his aid if they do repent, in vv. 22b-25 the song of repentance follows, with Yahweh's reply in 4.1-4 as the conclusion. We have exactly the same arrangement in Hos. 14.2-9: vv. 2, 3a, call to repentance; vv. 3b, 4, song of repentance; vv. 5-9, Yahweh's reply. It probably derives from the cult, where the priest as Yahweh's representative calls the people to repentance and gives them absolution afterwards. Instead of a complete song of lament we have here only a part of one, the repentance motif, in a somewhat expanded form, with a number of other motifs also quietly audible; in v. 22b, for example, the trust motif finds expression. Unlike the two songs mentioned previously, Yahweh's answer is not in this case negative but sounds favourable, like Hosea 14. It is a picture of the future which the prophet sees and in which he finds comfort. He sees realized in it his most heartfelt desire, that the people will humble themselves as a result of the judgment and then return in penitence to Yahweh, who will receive them with open arms. It is—and the same is also true of Hosea 14—an eschatological song of repentance', which explains why a more detailed description of the calamity is lacking (cf. 14.2ff., 19ff.).

| [79] Occasional echoes of the communal song of lament, especially of the lament and repentance motif, are found in 2.27bβ; 3.4f.; 8.14b, 19a, 20.[32] The authenticity of 10.23-25[33] on the other hand, is quite dubious, and 31.18f.[34] is also better disregarded.

Though the authenticity of some individual passages may be open to question, it is an established fact that Jeremiah used this song type. And this is all the more likely to be the case for the individual songs of lament which are so close to them in their whole structure, as in their vocabulary. It is in the nature of the matter that the communal songs of lament did not afford him an opportunity of expressing his personal experiences and feelings. Their purpose in any case was quite a different one. At best, the eschatological song serves him as a means of expressing his own hopes and longings; the other songs are aimed at the people and are intended to have a hortatory and admonitory effect on them. We shall therefore not expect any specially prophetic characteristics here.[35]

## 2. The Dependence of Jeremiah's Poems of Lament on the Songs of Lament Type

### a. The greater antiquity of the type
If, in conclusion, we must now clarify the relationship between the

psalms of Jeremiah and the songs of lament of the Psalter and decide the unavoidable question of priority and dependence, the situation has changed with respect to most earlier answers in that *it is no longer a question of the relationship of individual passages to one another but of agreement in the song type.* The essential thing is to explain the fact that the same type is present in both places, and there are only two possibilities on offer: either the song of lament type is older and has been manipulated by Jeremiah, or Jeremiah created the type and the psalms are dependent on him. To put it more simply: which is older, the literary type or Jeremiah?

| [80] It is not actually very likely that Jeremiah should have created the type; for 'types are not invented by individuals'.[36] Rather a literary type, i.e. a complex of individual pieces of literature which form an inner unity by means of a generally fixed content together with the forms usually chosen for it, comes into being where similar external circumstances repeatedly call for a similar phraseology, so that ultimately through the long process of repetition, all by itself, a certain style is formed, a stock of fixed expressions[37] and certain semi-fixed outward forms. It is of course *individuals* that stand at the very beginnings of the type. But one cannot designate one particular person or another who first turned to his God with a lament and a petition as creator of the type, any more than one can hold any custom to have been created by one of those who first performed the practice. For, just as the custom only comes about as a practice becomes established in a community of people, so too the type only comes about with the help of many, who express the same material repeatedly in a similar form. It is no more possible to ascertain the type's precise moment of birth and its originator or creator than it is those of a particular custom. But when a type can be so clearly made out as Jeremiah's can, it is bound to be common property already.

This general observation is confirmed by a series of specific points.

1. In the Psalms, the type appears as a rounded and self-contained whole. In Jeremiah, parts are sometimes missing, e.g. the invocation, and the structure is less transparent. It is clear from the factors mentioned under numbers 3 and 4 that this should not be interpreted as indicating that Jeremiah's psalms are the cruder, earlier stage from which the pure type then developed.

2. In the Psalms, the type is pure; in Jeremiah, a prophetic element is mixed in with it—an element which can easily be distinguished as alien to it.

3. The song of lament originally came into existence for cases of sickness, and this had a long-term effect on the linguistic usage. Jeremiah, too, occasionally speaks of wounds, blows, pains (10.19; 15.18), of healing (17.14), but always in a metaphorical sense. | [81]

4. The spiritual song of lament of the Psalter was in all probability preceded by an older cultic stage,[38] while Jeremiah's songs are fully 'spiritual'.

5. The song of lament is very closely associated with the thanksgiving song, which is able to look back upon distress and rescue. The two are as complementary as the two shells of a mussel, so that it is hardly conceivable that one should have come into being without the other. In the case, however, of Jeremiah, whose life offered little occasion to offer 'thanks', we have no more than a weak trace (20.13) of the thanksgiving song, which is, moreover, a long way removed from a complete thanksgiving song.

6. When elsewhere in the prophetic corpus lyrical types are to be found—viz., the dirge, the taunt-poem, the drinking song, the pilgrim song and many other types[39]—it is clear that they are modelled on song types prevalent among the people and that the prophets know how to make them serviceable for their own purposes. To assume that the prophets created all these song types themselves would be as absurd as regarding Goethe as the creator of the folk-song because he occasionally wrote poetry in the manner of the folk-song. And what applies there is only fair in the case of Jeremiah's poems of lament too.

All this compels us to look to *the literary type for the priority and to Jeremiah for the dependency.*

The fact that in many circles so little account is taken of this possibility is due largely to the fact that people are generally used to seeing the composition of the Psalms as no earlier than exilic or post-exilic. This may be the case for the majority of the Psalms in the tradition, but it does not exclude the possiblity that psalms composition itself is very much older. There have always been individual scholars who have strongly represented this view,[40] a view now confirmed by the findings of literary type research [*Gattungsforschung*].[41] The very assumption of an earlier stage in the cult, for which there is evidence in the older literature itself (Amos 5.23), leads us into the pre-exilic period. And there are other signs here and there which indicate that songs of lament existed already in earlier times. In the song of lament of Ps. 28, for example, it says in

v. 8 that Yahweh is a protection for his people and a shield for his anointed one, which obviously refers to the reigning king. | [82] Ps. 61 contains (vv. 7f.[6f.]) a petition for the king; this is inserted between the assurance of being heard and the vow, thus obviously an addition, but from the time when there was still a king. Similarly in Ps. 63 the mention of the king (v. 11aα) interrupts the context, and the same applies to the petition for the king in Ps. 84.8f. These are all additions which actually belong to the end of the song, where we do indeed, in some psalms find a patriotic petition like this for the king or the people, or for both together (Pss. 3.8[7]; 14.7; 25.22; 28.8f.; 29.11; 125.5; 1 Sam. 2.10b). In some cases the petition has clearly been added later, while in others it may always have formed the song's conclusion.

The royal thanksgiving song, Ps. 18, which probably dates from the last decades of the southern kingdom, but which in its broad conception takes a relatively late place within its type, presupposes a song of lament in v. 6 and in a number of other expressions (vv. 4f., 16-19) has points of contact with our songs of lament.[42]

The occurrence of the same song type among the great neighbouring states to the East and West also speaks for the great antiquity of the Israelite songs of lament.

*Babylonian-Assyrian* songs of lament have been preserved in great numbers so that we are able to form quite a clear picture of them today.[43] A well-known song to Ishtar,[44] for example, has the following structure: lines 1-41, hymnic introduction; 42-55, petition; 56-78, lament; 79-92, petition; 93-94, lament; 95-100, petition; 101-102, vow; 103-105, content of the vow in the form of a thanksgiving song. The components are thus essentially the same as those in the Israelite psalms. Generally speaking, the Assyrian songs differ from them only in their greater length and in their replacement of the 'invocation' by the hymnic introduction,[45] which is very common, even forcing the lament sometimes into the background.[46] But these differences appear peripheral | [83] in relation to the agreement in the whole conception. As in Israel, the occasion for the prayer is, in most cases, illness, along with persecution and suffering of other kinds. In the lament in particular the points of contact extend to matters of detail, e.g. the painful 'how long',[47] the complaint that even the singer's closest relations want nothing more to do with him,[48] the description of his wretched existence, his weeping and lamenting.[49] Nor are the repentance[50] and innocence motifs[51] lacking.

The particular value to us of the Assyrian and Babylonian songs of lament lies in the fact that their setting in life can be clearly discerned. The connection with the cult, which in the Israelite case can only be arrived at by deduction, is only in evidence here. Appended to the songs are often details of the administration of sacrifices and the invocation ceremony, of the clothing of the penitent etc. Not infrequently, alongside the supplicant the priest appears, who invokes the deity and mediates his reply; in such cases a formal dialogue can develop between the two.[52]

In other respects, too, we are given various insights into the development of the literary type. As in Israel, so here also are found both communal and personal songs of lament, which in the main are similarly structured.[53] But while in Israel they stand next to each other, quite independently of one another here there are many indications that the personal ones have emerged from the communal ones.[54] For the communal song is often spoken by the king, and, since the fate of the country is also dependent on the well-being of the king, it is easy for the communal song to become an individual one, and in fact most of the individual songs of lament are placed on the lips of the king.[55] We have songs which are on the border between communal and individual.[56] Then, as it became possible for an ordinary man to take the king's place, the song became more and more generalized; in the end, it was possible for any name to be inserted.[57] In the case of the communal songs of lament, the occasions for which—flood, pestilence, lunar eclipse, | [84] war emergency etc.—were always roughly the same, in the course of the years particular set patterns evolved, which were preserved in the temple archives and could with minor alterations and additions be used again and again;[58] the same may be assumed in the case of the individual songs too.[59]

In *Egypt*, no true songs of lament have yet been found, though thanksgiving songs have, on votive tablets, which look back on the distress that has been survived, and in so doing quote the lament song of that time.[60] The last two strophes of the longest of these songs runs:[61]

9  He says:[62] 'If the servant was ready(?) to sin,
    so the Lord is ready(?) to be merciful.
  The Lord of Thebes is not angry all the day;
    if he is angry, (it is only) for a moment, and
    nothing of it remains.

> (The anger) is turned upon us in mercy,
>> Amon returns(?) with(?) his breath of air.
> As thou livest, thou wilt be merciful,
>> and what(?) happily has been averted
>> will not return.'

10          He says:[62] 'I will make this stele to thy name,
>> I will immortalize this song on it as an epigraph,
> if thou savest Necht-Amon, the scribe, for me.
> I spoke thus and thou didst hear me!
>> Now behold, I am doing what I said!
> Thou art the protector of him who calls upon thee,
>> who rejoices in the right, thou, Lord of Thebes.'

Strophe 9 contains the meditations with which the poet comforted himself during his son's sickness: he trusted in the mercy of the deity, finally lifting himself up to the assurance of being heard. Strophe 10 mentions the vow which he then spoke, namely to inscribe the song he has just sung on a stele as an everlasting memorial, which is what he is now doing. Trust motif, assurance of being heard, vow—all these are also parts of the Israelite song of lament.

Another song describes the distress of that time, which the singer had incurred by his sin.[63] | [85]

> I was a man who swore wickedly by Ptah, the
>> Lord of Truth,
>> and he caused me to see darkness in the daytime.
>
> He made me to be like the animals in the street
>> while I was in his land.
> He caused men and gods to watch after(?) me,
>> while I was like a man doing abominable things
>>> against his lord.
> Ptah, the Lord of Wisdom, is just towards me,
>> after(?) he has punished me.
> Be merciful to me, that(?) I may see how(?)
>> merciful thou art, etc.

Scant though these traces are, they still allow the conclusion that in Egypt too there were lament and thanksgiving songs which are very close in structure to the Israelite ones.

The greater antiquity of these Babylonian and Egyptian parallels is easy to demonstrate. We possess, for example, a royal song of lament by Ashurbanipal II (c. 1000 BC). Preserved in Ashurbanipal's library is also the 'song of the suffering righteous man', which, though its complex construction means it cannot be called a song of lament without further qualification, certainly presupposes such songs, and perhaps thanksgiving songs, too, in the third tablet; its language, which has already required philological commentary, and the various copies and duplicates of it, similarly lead one to suspect its considerably greater antiquity.[64] The steles of the Theban necropolis, which bear the aforementioned thanksgiving songs, date from the thirteenth and twelfth centuries.

Now, despite the differences, the agreement between these songs and the Israelite ones is so extensive that the assumption of a connection between them can hardly be avoided, which is true not only of the songs of lament but of psalms composition *per se*.[65] But the only conceivable kind of connection would be that the Israelite poetry, being younger, is dependent on that of its older neighbours. Since the Israelite songs, aside from certain terms proper to court style, show no signs of a foreign background, and since they have experienced a development in Israel itself, the borrowing must have begun at quite an early stage. Presumably, alongside the other products of Babylonian and Egyptian culture which the Israelites in Canaan | [86] adopted at the sanctuaries, they also adopted the various types of communal and individual cultic poetry.[66]

## b. *The adoption of the type by Jeremiah*

It is easy to understand how Jeremiah came to adopt the song of lament form in particular. Like none of his predecessors, the man with the gentle, sensitive disposition suffered, under his profession and his prophetic compulsion. Not only was it painful to him that he had to announce their downfall to his own people, whom he still loved in spite of their corruption—which was something his predecessors did not always find easy either. He suffered at least as much from the fact that his life was now a great, ceaseless struggle, that in his work for Yahweh his reward was nothing but scorn and mockery, even severe persecution, that his clairvoyance, which showed him the horrors of the future as if in the present, stopped him enjoying life's harmless pleasures, and that he had to stand so completely alone and without joy in life. It often seemed to him almost as if the whole course of his life was going to be futile, as if Yahweh was leaving him in the lurch after he had given everything for him. And yet again and again he was won over by his God, so that he took upon himself anew the onerous, wearing ministry. His great poetic bent meant he could not help giving expression to all these crushing troubles, in order to give his tormented heart some relief. The prophets before him had not felt all this quite as deeply as he, so that the prophetic style did not really offer him an appropriate medium of expression. So he took hold of that type of song which came closest to his experiences and feelings, the individual song of lament.

> This type attracted the prophet because the lament and the comfort of the individual soul resounded in it. The heart of these lament-singers is full of pain and sorrow; his surely too! They complain particularly about their physical suffering; his hurt is that Yahweh's words are still not being fulfilled. They are surrounded by enemies who doubt their righteousness; how many enemies he has on account of his prophesying! They finally lift themselves to the assurance that God will hear them and cause them to triumph, but send terrible ruin upon their opponents; to him, God himself declares that he will hold him fast | [87] and overthrow his slanderers! [67]

In this way the song of lament was transferred to circumstances which, despite all the external similarities, were of a completely different order. Hitherto intended for external suffering, especially of a physical nature, it now has to express deep spiritual pain too. This could be no more than an incomplete success, and all sorts of abuses were found to creep in—which is why the songs were so seldom correctly understood. Precisely the finest feelings could not find expression. The song of lament style lies like a thick veil over what is actually intended to be said. Sometimes the expressions that have been taken over sound so general that nothing at all concrete can be learnt from them (e.g. 45.3), or they are meant to be taken purely metaphorically like the expressions for physical suffering. What is said about mockery and persecution is more concrete, but does not in itself take us any further than the experiences of the psalmists. The most personal words, of course, are those which mirror the prophetic experience and sensibility. But such passages are relatively few in number, so that even here not too much enlightenment can be gained as to the circumstances that actually underlie the songs. We have to depend on conjectures and reconstructions on the basis of the few indications we have. Much must remain unsure. In particular, concerning the external circumstances and the time of original composition we learn practically nothing. This is quite under-standable. As these songs only deal with his own most personal experiences, in the nature of the matter there are no allusions to external or political events, which alone could serve us as reference points. And where events in his environment do have a role to play they are of a quite apolitical nature, such as instances of mockery and persecution involving only a few people; these are no help to us either. One has to be very wary of trying to relate completely apolitical statements like his sitting alone (15.17) or his weeping in private (13.17) to particular political situations. A certain twilight thus necessarily remains over these songs, which all future research will scarcely be able to illuminate wholly either. The reason for this lies simply in their peculiar, mixed style.

| [88] We find a similar mixture of styles, to a much weaker degree to be sure, only with the prophet *Habakkuk*. The very first of his songs (1.2-4) runs thus:

| 2 | How long have I cried, Yahweh, |   |
|---|---|---|
|   | and thou hearest not; | (5) |
|   | have I cried to thee: 'Violence!' |   |
|   | and thou helpest not? | (5) |
| 3 | Why dost thou make me see trouble, |   |
|   | must I look upon ill,[68] | (5) |
|   | Are violence and oppression before me |   |
|   | and does contention make uproar?[69] | (5) |
| 4 | Therefore the law becomes feeble |   |
|   | and justice does not take its course;[70] | (5) |
|   | For the wicked encircles the righteous— |   |
|   | therefore[71] justice is so perverted! | (3 + 3) |

The echoes of the psalmic style עד־אנה, למה, זעק, שוע—stand out clearly. Whenever these were recognized, however, this usually led to a denial of the prophetic authorship of the verses.[72] But שׁד itself speaks for a prophetic origin, for it is a word that is so seldom encountered outside prophetic linguistic usage.[73] The verses are anyway quite understandable in the repertoire of a prophet. They are strongly reminiscent of Jer. 20.8, where Jeremiah complains about the injustice done to him. Here, however, the concern is rather with all and any injustice that the prophet sees. He can never simply walk past unconcerned when he sees something unjust. He has to intervene or lodge a complaint. But when this is constantly repeated it is itself a reason for the people to see him as ridiculous and a nuisance, and the bad situation remains unchanged. The prophet feels this; but no more can he change himself for that, and so his indignation is aroused again every time. Listening to this lament we can clearly hear the sensitive, almost nervous-sounding human being.

Rather less personal is the next song of lament (1.12-17), a complaint that the ungodly hold sway and oppress the righteous. Reminiscent of the psalmic style once more is למה in v. 13, | [89] and הלעולם, which is to be read in v. 17 (cf. Pss. 77.8; 85.6). Yahweh's reply then follows in 2.1-3, which, in the way it is introduced (cf. Isa. 21.6), vouches for the prophetic origin of the whole song.

All the features we have mentioned—the use made of the song of lament style, the juxtaposition of lament and divine reply, and the pronounced, lyrical sensitivity—put Habakkuk quite close to Jeremiah,[74] whose younger contemporary in fact he seems to have been. A likely explanation of the simultaneous appearance of two figures who are so closely related in this respect is that individualism *per se* was developing particularly strongly at that period. This does not, however, rule out the possibility that in respect of form Habakkuk was directly dependent on Jeremiah. But however close the relationship, Jeremiah still emerges as the vastly richer and more profound character.

Out of the deep sorrow of this rich life, what is basically a completely new song type has been born. The subjective, lyrical impulse that was thereby introduced into prophetic poetry meant an enrichment and deepening of it with respect to its human side. The natural, human feelings which in the older prophets were all but totally supressed, now come to the fore. If hitherto the human Ego seemed to be submerged in the personality of the deity, so that prophetic speech was almost completely controlled by the feeling and mood of the deity,[75] now it gains life of its own. While hitherto one could only see the prophet, now one also sees the human being.

We can thus draw for ourselves a much richer and clearer picture of Jeremiah than of his predecessors. Of the personal circumstances of an Amos and an Isaiah we know only just so much as is connected with their public prophetic activity. Even Hosea only narrates the tragedy of his marriage because for him it has assumed symbolic significance. It is first of all with Jeremiah that we meet reflection on his prophetic ministry and the sorrows that it entails. The dichotomy between human desire and prophetic compulsion may not have been foreign to the earlier prophets either; but Jeremiah with his tender disposition feels it much more keenly and is thus able to give it such poignant expression. In his case, too, the individualism is, to begin with, rather more than simply religious. He would like to be as the others and be able to live, and his natural zest for life asserts itself; the way he takes the lot of the great man | [90] and the pain of having to stand alone and away from the others seems to have quite a modern ring about it. But it is in vain that he stands up to his God. He succumbs to his might over and over again, becoming chained all the more closely to him. The individualism then becomes a religious individualism, and the prophet enters a new and much more personal relationship with his God. For the latter is the only thing left to him in life; he has had to part with everything else. There must have been times when even this consolation threatened to disappear, times to which we owe some of the most beautiful songs. But we cannot believe that this was the end of it for him.

### c. *Jeremiah's poetic individuality*
When research has come to a recognition of the mixture of styles in the psalms of Jeremiah, its task is to ascertain as accurately as possible what features of these songs are due to the style of the song of lament and what is Jeremiah's own creation. Often when there is resistance to research on literary types the particular cause is the fear that it might undermine the individuality of the poets.[76] Precisely the opposite should be the case. It is only with the aid of this kind of research that in our case, for example, we can tell where the individuality of the prophet in fact begins; otherwise it is easy to look for it in the wrong place. For it begins only *where we find deviations, in form or content, from the style of the psalms.* Cornill, for example, complains that the strange images in Jer. 14.7-9 are now supposed to be nothing but 'schema'.[77] Sellin[78] correctly replies that 14.7, 8a, 9b are indeed modelled on given forms, while the nucleus, vv. 8b, 9a, is a marvellous and highly original creation of Jeremiah's. The point is, however, that Yahweh's oracle in v. 10 proclaims *wrath* rather than the customary *consolation*; Jeremiah's originality is shown precisely in the way that he first of all follows the popular form, only to slap it suddenly in the face. (This sudden reversal in the oracle is found also in 12.5f.; 15.1f., 19ff.) There are many examples of this sort, as I endeavoured to show in the examination of the individual songs, above; we shall reiterate some of this at this point. Jeremiah

intensified the traditional picture of the sacrificial lamb (11.19). He transformed the innocence motif into lament (15.17). He made space for the wild pain that | [91] ravaged his heart in those complaints and reproaches, parallels to which would be sought in vain in the Psalter (15.10, 18a; 20.7, 14ff.). His are the drastic images with which he pictures the deity's overcoming of him (20.7) and letting him down (15.18b; cf. 14.8b, 9a). His is the skill of pouring the personal experiences in his life as a prophet into the song of lament mould, thereby filling it with new content. Above all, his is the skill of creating a kind of dialogue between human being and God by combining this prophetic song of lament with the oracle—a dialogue in which he was able to set down the most profound religious insight as it came to him in times of great suffering.

These may be the most important examples of the outworkings of his poetic individuality. And then, in addition, the fullness and depth of his thoughts, rising so high above the average of the psalms, the warmth of natural, human sensibility, the greatness of his passion, the sincerity and humility of religious experience. In comparison with this, what will it matter if we can no longer regard the pattern of his psalms and a good part of their vocabulary as created by him! We have gained more and better things than what is hereby lost. It is only now that we recognize what he had before him and what he made of it that we can properly assess his accomplishment. And he is certainly not a lesser person to us than if we looked at him in the old way!

We shall not, of course, manage to make this clear-cut distinction at all points, above all because the songs of lament that we have are probably all younger than Jeremiah. And though their more ancient antecedents should not have differed from them to any great degree, we have no certainty regarding individual cases, with which we are mainly concerned. Indeed we must even reckon with the possibility that Jeremiah's songs, precisely because of their psalmic character, may have influenced the later psalms composition. So it is not inconceivable—and this is quite compatible with the priority of the literary type as such—that some individual Psalms passages may possibly imitate passages in Jeremiah, or that expressions coined by Jeremiah may have been taken over into the language of the Psalms. Duhm and Cornill, for example, have expressed the conjecture that Jeremiah coined the expression 'Yahweh, who tries the heart and the kidneys' (11.20; 20.12). It would be worth considering, too whether the exclamation 'terror on every side', which occurs in a purely prophetic song in Jeremiah (6.25) may not have been transferred from Jeremiah into the psalm (31.14); our finding, however, was that more probably the words in the corresponding passage in Jeremiah (20.10) have been introduced | [92] from the psalm—both Jeremiah and the psalm may have adopted the cry from another source. In view of the peculiar relationship between the sources no certainty can be attained, and my conjecture in this direction can be countered by the opposite claim, with at least as much justification. Thus if Jeremiah's songs did in fact influence psalms composition, in time the prophetic aspects completely lost their contours, and the remainder was simply absorbed into the psalms style, so that our eyes can no longer make it out.

The relationship of Jeremiah's songs of lament to the Psalms is thus considerably more complex than appeared from earlier attempts at a solution. In the main, precisely the oldest view, the one least clouded by criticism, namely that Jeremiah is dependent on the Psalms, has turned out to be correct. In no way—this must be expressly stated— does this mean a victory of traditionalism over criticism. In the course of its development science often proceeds in mysterious ways. And when it has apparently arrived back at an earlier position, it has in fact come a lot further nonetheless; for it now finds itself—to use the metaphor of a spiral staircase—a whole storey higher. In asserting Jeremiah's dependence on the Psalms today we mean something quite different from what was understood by this fifty years ago. For us it is no longer a matter of the prophets' dependence on *individual psalms* but on the *psalms style*. Our position is in principle further removed from the former view than from others who in their criticism always maintained a correct, if one-sided observation. And precisely that view which disputed the authenticity of the songs, which our study has been primarily concerned to oppose, has without doubt done greater justice to the psalmic character of the songs than those which sought priority in Jeremiah by giving attention principally to the prophetic side of those songs. Thus in the end each view has furthered research in its own way and prepared the ground for a solution that seeks to do justice to all these factors. Even the wrong turnings in science are all, in the last analysis, stages in its forward progress.

# NOTES

## Notes to Chapter 1

1. Cf. Fr. Baethgen, *ZAW* 5 (1885), p. 99.
2. Cf. T.K. Cheyne, *The Origin and Religious Contents of the Psalter* (1891), pp. 122, 136.
3. Cf. Cheyne, *op. cit.*, p. 135; I have not had access to the book.
4. His essay, 'The Book of Jeremiah', in *The New World* 9 (1900), pp. 655-73, was not accessible to me.
5. I do not wish to deny that certain beginnings in such research were already being made before Gunkel, especially in the field of the Psalms. But those early attempts were not so comprehensive, and in particular they remained without significance for the question treated here.
6. In one respect W. Caspari's essay, 'Jeremia als Redner und Selbst-beobachter' [Jeremiah as Orator and Introvert], *NKZ* 26 (1915), pp. 777-88 and 842-63, belongs here, a work which did not come to my notice until my study was virtually completed. Caspari never refers to Gunkel and only occasionally to Balla; he works with the same literary types although in matters of detail he often is not incisive enough—and also arrives at more or less the same conclusion.

## Notes to Chapter 2

1. Cf. H. Gunkel, *Die israelitische Literatur* (1906), pp. 65, 88f.; *RGG*, IV, cols. 1945-47; *Ausgewählte Psalmen* (3rd edn, 1912); E. Balla, *op. cit.*, pp. 13-29, 47-56; H. Schmidt, *Die religiöse Lyrik im AT* (1912), pp. 16-27; W. Staerk, *op. cit.*, pp. 143-228.

In order to prevent misunderstandings it should be noted here that I follow Gunkel's terminology throughout. Thus, by 'songs of lament' (*Klagelieder*) I mean that type of psalm that is often designated 'psalms of lament' (*Klagepsalmen*), while Staerk and Kittel have introduced the expression 'petitions' (*Bittgebete*) and in some cases also 'consolations' (*Trostgebete*). The term 'dirge' (*Leichenklage*) then remains for the Hebrew 'Qina'.

The various texts cited largely follow available translations of the Psalms.

2. The 'song of lament' (*Klagelied*) in 27.7-14 should probably be separated from the 'psalm of trust' (*Vertrauenspsalm*), 27.1-6; cf. Balla, p. 16.

3. Ps. 31 can probably be divided into two songs of lament, vv. 2-9 and vv. 10-25[1-8, 9-24]; cf. Balla, p. 16.

4. Pss. 9 and 10 together form an alphabetical poem, which, however, is not very homogeneous in content; cf. Balla, pp. 111f.

5. With Saadja, Ewald and others I read חֲכִי.

6. Cf. K. Budde, *Hiob* [Job] (2nd edn, 1913), *ad loc.*

7. Reading כעשן, following manuscripts and G T (Duhm, Kittel).

8. Text follows BH.

9. Job 6.14f. seems already to be protesting against this; cf. Budde, *ad loc.*

10. On the following, cf. Gunkel, *RGG*, III, cols. 2357ff.

11. Cf. Gunkel, *Ausgewählte Psalmen* (3rd edn), pp. 4f.

12. With G S, גל is to be vocalized as a perfect (Olshausen).

13. From 37.5 it seems על should be read.

14. Cf. also 31.11, where it seems that instead of מאר a term synonymous with חרפה should be read, such as מורא (Duhm).

15. Following the text of BH, cf. Budde, *ad loc.*

16. For נינם יחד read נכחידם (Budde, *ZAW* 35 [1915], p. 190).

17. Unless גוי simply means 'people' here (Duhm and others).

18. On this, cf. Balla, pp. 22f. It would admittedly be conceivable that the reference is to Jews in the Diaspora.

19. Cf. Cheyne, *Origin and Rel. Contents of the Psalter*, p. 135; Sellin, *Disputatio*, pp. 118f.

20. Cf. Gunkel, *Ausgewählte Psalmen* (3rd edn), pp. 291ff.

21. On the history of these terms cf. R. Kittel, *Die Psalmen* (1914), pp. 315-18.

22. עניתי (Thrupp, in Delitzsch, *ad loc.*).

23. The mood reflected in these verbs is clearly seen in Job 6.20, for example. In Jer. 2.26, בשת is used for the caught thief.

24. Following G. (Duhm, Budde).

25. Cf. above, pp. 22f.

26. Cf. Balla (p. 22) and Kittel (*Psalmen*, pp. 237-39), who however takes too little account of the connection with sickness.

27. ענני for עלי (Bevan).

28. Cf. Gunkel, *Ausgewählte Psalmen* (3rd edn), p. 128.

29. תחלת, following GS.

30. The verbs used here, בחן and צרף, are taken from the goldsmiths' trade; cf. Isa. 40.19; 48.10; Zech. 13.9; Job. 23.10.

31. In such cases we must always reckon with the additional possibility that a more thorough self-examination has in fact led to the conscience dealing with untruths inherent in the singer's former sense of innocence.

32. Cf. Gunkel, *Ausgewählte Psalmen* (3rd edn), pp. 71f., 84, 86; Kittel, *Psalmen*, pp. 106-108.

33. 30 is a thanksgiving song; but it quotes the original song of lament in vv. 9-11[8-10].

34. יקח is to be translated like a perfect. In Hebrew poetry the usual imperfect seems often to render the past tense; cf. e.g. Pss. 8.6[5]; 21.4, 6[3, 5]; 81.8, 13[7, 12]; 92.12[11]; 105.40; 106.12, 17, 19; 107.6, 13f., 26f., 33-35; 118.10-12; 114.3; Exod. 15.16; Isa. 12.1, etc.

35. I delete ויבשו.

36. Caspari (*op. cit.*, p. 846) enumerates a series of further passages in this connection, but these are drawn from all the other possible psalm types, which there is little point in mentioning. In the song of lament only the three passages cited are to be found, and the first two of these are taken from communal songs of lament.

37. אמתך for מאתך (Graetz).

38. Text according to BH.

39. לְעַנּוֹת (Gunkel, *Ausgewählte Psalmen* [3rd edn], p. 302).

40. Cf. Balla, pp. 29ff.

41. This does not of course exclude the possibility of making rearrangements in some individual cases; the uncertainty in the transmission of the text makes this perfectly justifiable.

42. Cf. Gunkel, *Die israelitische Literatur*, p. 65.

43. Cf. below, pp. 92f.

44. Cf. Gunkel, *Ausgewählte Psalmen* (3rd edn), pp. 49f.

45. Cf. above, p. 21.

46. Cf. Balla, pp. 26f.


## Notes to Chapter 3

1. Here I have used the commentaries of Cornill (1905), Driver (1906), Duhm (1901), Erbt (1902), Ewald (2nd edn, 1868), Giesebrecht (2nd edn, 1907), Graf (1862), Hitzig (1841), C.F. Keil (1872), Köberle (1908), von Orelli (3rd edn, 1905), J.W. Rothstein (in Kautzsch, I, 3rd edn, 1910), H. Schmidt (1915), and also A.B. Ehrlich, *Randglossen zum AT*, IV [Marginal notes on the OT] (1912).

In the translation of the texts the figure in brackets at the end of the line signifies the number of metrical feet in the original text (as Sievers does), while (3) indicates the trimeter, (4) the tetrameter, (5) the pentameter (the so-called Qina verse), (3 + 3) the double trimeter, (6) the hexameter (2 + 2 + 2), (7) the heptameter (3 + 4 or 4 + 3), (4 + 4) the octameter or double tetrameter.

On principle I have been reticent in making textual changes on metric grounds, in particular I could not decide to press one and the same metre throughout the whole of a poem, since I felt the facts did not justify this.

In this chapter the references from the book of Jeremiah are not usually prefixed by the designation (Jer.). I give the texts not quite in the traditional sequence, assembling in the appendix (pp. 63ff.) those which stand somewhat further removed from the lament songs.

2. Cf. below, p. 45.

3. On this, cf. Cornill.

4. Cf. p. 36.

5. Here, אלהים should be deleted (Baethgen, Kittel).

6. Cf. Duhm, Hölscher.

7. See above, p. 31.

8. It does not tell against our deletion of הבחורים that only the daughters would then appear as representatives of those who stay at home; for the young men would be out in the field in any case.

9. For example by Stade, who however was later inclined to re-accept its genuineness (see above, p. 15), by Duhm and by Hölscher (p. 394).

10. Erbt, p. 172.

11. So H. Schmidt, p. 235.

12. Budde, *Geschichte der althebräischen Literatur* (1906), pp. 136f., H. Schmidt, p. 234.

13. Erbt, p. 172; Davidson in Hastings' *Dictionary of the Bible*, II (1899), p. 573a.

14. הוציא in this sense is usually combined with 'out of the mouth' or 'out of the heart'; absolutely, as here, it is otherwise found only in Eccl. 5.2, where, however, 'your heart' is the subject.

15. Cf. BH.

16. Cf. above, p. 30.

17. Text according to BH.

18. Giesebrecht, Rothstein and H. Schmidt read the text in this way. But it would actually follow from this that one should also stay with MT for v. 16aα.

19. Erbt, p. 177.

20. The expression is otherwise used only of the ark, the temple, the city of Jerusalem and the people, and in Amos 9.12 also of the vanquished peoples; cf. Fr. Giesebrecht, *Die alttestamentliche Schätzung des Gottesnamens* (1901) [The OT Estimation of the Divine Name], pp. 21f.; W. Heitmüller, *Im Namen Jesu* [In the Name of Jesus] (1903), pp. 171ff. In reference to an individual, one can hardly imagine its use for anyone but a prophet.

21. Cf. Schiller's Kassandra:

> Alles um mich lebt und liebt—
> Mir nur ist das Herz betrübt.

> All around me live and love—
> Only my heart is so sad.

22. Caspari agrees, p. 852.

23. In the only passage where this does not apply (Hos. 7.16) the text seems to be corrupt.

24. J. Pedersen (*Der Eid bei den Semiten* [The Oath among the Semites] [1914], p. 81) translates our passage: 'you filled me with trouble, with curse'. But his justification, 'Jeremiah is not angry but unhappy', is inappropriate; for as a prophet he is also angry at the people's sin.

25. את חמת יהוה מלאתי. It is surely no coincidence that our passage reads מלאתני; it is intended to be a gentle reproach against Yahweh. The text of G, 'I am filled', is much paler. The same applies to Caspari's suggestion (p. 852) that זעם should be taken as the subject: 'anger fills me, namely with evils and troubles'; one would then have to supply the main point oneself.

26. How Caspari (p. 857) can find the 'plea for rescue' here, I cannot comprehend.

27. Ehrlich's emendation to רצח, 'murderous', rests on a misunderstanding of the style of the psalm. His reference to Ps. 42.10 is of no help since בר צח should certainly be read (Gunkel).

28. As Cornill does. Caspari (p. 852) also feels the need to protect Jeremiah against an accusation of irreverence: 'The defamatory expression is contained only in a simile, so God is not charged with lying'.

29. Hölscher also cites this passage but without indicating what he thinks it proves. Surely not the literary dependence of the Jeremiah passage?

30. Cf. Gunkel, in H. Schmidt, p. li; similarly, Num. 24.17ff.; Isa. 7.14ff.; 8.6ff.; 13; 17.12-14; 21.1-10 etc.

31. Cf. also Hölscher, p. 26!

32. The verses agree with 1.18f. The usual practice is to ask in which passage they are genuine and then to decide in favour either of ch. 1 (Hölscher) or ch. 15 (Mowinckel, p. 20 n. 1). But in the former context they are protected by v. 17, and in the latter a comforting conclusion is desirable after v. 19. We are dealing with an idea that may well have preoccupied Jeremiah on many occasions. Both passages are authentic, but have become contaminated with one another at a later stage.

33. The expression רעים seems to be particularly at home in the wisdom literature (Prov. 4.14; 12.12; 14.19; 15.3, 15; Sir. 4.20; 11.33; 12.6f.; 41.5).

34. According to N. Schmidt (*Encyclopaedia Biblica*, II, p. 2389), the speaker in this song is not an individual, but the people (Zion). In the light of our study, this interpretation founders already on v. 17.

35. Ehrlich is, it seems, correct to understand מחתה in this way; cf. יחתו, v. 18.

36. Throne of honour, 14.21 (cf. Ps. 47.9); height, Ezek. 20.40; place of the sanctuary, Isa. 60.13; hope of Israel, 14.8.

37. Cf. below, pp. 92f.

38. Stade, N. Schmidt, Hölscher, p. 399.

39. Cornill, Duhm, Ehrlich, Erbt, Giesebrecht.

40. A glorification of the deity and the sanctuary together is also found in the introduction of the eschatological Ps. 48.1f.

41. Balla (p. 56) and H. Schmidt (pp. 269f.) support their authenticity; cf. also Mowinckel (3rd edn, p. 20).

42. Duhm's emendation to תוחלתי is quite unnecessary.

43. Cf. above, p. 22.

44. For the same reason, Giesebrecht thinks it necessary to alter the text to אויה דברו יבאנו, 'woe! his word comes upon us', thereby losing the whole point.

45. Cf. Erbt, p. 181.

46. Cf. also Ps. 7.

47. For עקב I read עמק, following G; cf. Ps. 64.7 (J.D. Michaelis, Hitzig, Cornill, Duhm and others).

48. I delete מכל (Cornill, Duhm).

49. ובחן, in accordance with the translations.

50. Verse 10b (= 32.19bβ) cannot be authentic in our passage (Cornill, Duhm), since v. 10a does not speak of an outward change but of the hidden thoughts of the heart.

51. Such is the suggestion of Mowinckel (p. 20 n. 2).

52. Gunkel, in H. Schmidt, pp. lxixf.

53. Gunkel.

54. Most recent scholars delete the אל, following G; taken in the way suggested above, however, it does not cause the least offence. Albrecht Ritschl has understood the verse correctly, and in the preface to the third volume of *Rechtfertigung und Versöhnung* [Justification and Reconciliation] (2nd edn) has pointed it out to his opponents.

55. עמד לפני as in 15.19, cf. above, p. 50.

56. When Hölscher paraphrases v. 20: 'The speaker boasts that in his prayers before Yahweh he has spoken only good of his enemies', he overlooks that this in itself is an intercession. Also Caspari's understanding (*op. cit.*, pp. 858f.). 'The speaker is in 18.20b really saying no more than that he has complied impartially with the demands of his role in the cult, so that it was also effective for those who have now become his enemies'—does not do justice to the wording of the text.

57. Cf. e.g. 4.30f.; 13.18-27; 22.18f.; 25.32-38.

58. I should like to leave open the question whether Jeremiah is here really keeping to a psalms type that was created for the use of the community's dignitaries against the backsliders (Caspari, p. 859).

59. It is quite unnecessary even to delete just vv. 21, 22a (Erbt, H. Schmidt); v. 22b follows on from v. 22a at least as well as from v. 20, so that there is no question of an interruption of the context.

60. Cf. above, p. 55.

61. Cf. above, p. 25.

62. Cf. above, p. 44.

63. Cf. above, p. 47.

64. Cf. Isa. 13.2; 22.1; 40.6; 63.1; Jer. 46.3; Hos. 5.8; Ps. 2.1; and see

Gunkel, *Ausgewählte Psalmen* (3rd edn), pp. 9f., 15, and in H. Schmidt, pp. liif.

65. Cf. below, pp. 73ff.

66. So also Steuernagel, *Lehrbuch der Einleitung in das AT* [Textbook Introduction to the OT] (1912), p. 550.

67. Cf. most recently Mowinckel, pp. 14ff., 65f.

68. So also Erbt, Rothstein, H. Schmidt.

69. N. Schmidt reads הַגִּידוּ לְנְגִידֵנוּ and then also relates the יפתה to the נגיד. Quite unnecessarily; cf. Obad. 1.

70. Cf. above, p. 24.

71. Ehrlich even feels bound to make a textual emendation: אותי כגבור יריץ, 'He makes me run like a hero!'

72. Cornill, Duhm; cf. also Staerk, *op. cit.*, p. 153. The only real argument against the genuineness of the verse is that v. 11 is a good conclusion and that v. 12 is itself an appendage. But this is not convincing.

73. Gunkel, *Die israelitische Literatur*, p. 89.

74. Cf. above, p. 27.

75. Cf. Gunkel in *RGG*, III, cols. 493ff.

76. We also find it in Jer. 31.29, but the authenticity of Jer. 30–31 is very much in doubt, because the whole collection of 30.4–31.26 was originally anonymous and was only later connected to the rest of the book of Jeremiah by means of 30.1-3 and 31.27f. (cf. Mowinckel, pp. 45ff.).

77. Cf. the consistent explanation of the fall of Judah on the basis of the sins of Manasseh.

78. Cf. Job 9.2f. with 4.17.

79. Cornill, Duhm and others; Mowinckel (p. 29 n. 1) again argues for their authenticity.

80. אתך may not of course be deleted (against Rothstein), it should not be linked to the verb but the noun; cf. Ps. 78.37 (Ehrlich).

81. Entirely failing to recognize this psalm style, Ehrlich wants to change the 1st sg. suffixes into 3rd pl. and relate them to the previously mentioned wicked.

82. Caspari also (pp. 857, 859) takes too little account of the fact that the future expectation evident in these songs must first be sharply distinguished from his proclamation of salvation and disaster.

83. The 'how long' is reminiscent of the psalms of lament; cf. above, pp. 27f. The whole verse would fit just as well in a communal song of lament.

84. Guthe, in Kautzsch (3rd edn), II, p. 6.

85. Giesebrecht.

86. Cornill, Caspari, p. 845.

87. Cf. below, pp. 71f.

88. Cf. e.g. 5.7ff. after 5.1-6, where the prophet himself was speaking, and 12.7ff.; 17.1ff.; 22.20ff.

89. Similitude *e contrario*, as in Jer. 8.7; *4 Ezra* 9.34.

90. A. Jülicher, *Die Gleichnisreden Jesu* [The Parables of Jesus], I (2nd edn, 1899), p. 86 . From the NT compare Mt. 13.44ff.; Mk 3.23ff.; Lk. 5.36f.; 14.28ff.; 15.1ff.

91. *A maiori ad minus*: Prov. 15.11; Sir. 17.31.

92. For the question addressed to the hearers cf. also Isa. 5.3f.; *4 Ezra* 4.18; Mt. 21.31, 40f.; Lk. 7.43; 10.36f.

93. In this respect, Caspari (p. 854 n. 1) correctly objects to Balla's view (p. 55) that Jeremiah takes it upon himself to pronounce an oracle.

94. Gunkel, in Kautzsch, *Die Apokryphen und Pseudepigraphen des AT*, II (1900), p. 341.

95. Similarly, Caspari (p. 847): 'In a passage where otherwise consent is always being given, 12.5f. presents a No. In short the text is. . . such a remarkable thing that, if it had been transmitted anonymously somewhere people would now be searching for its author, seeking a quite extraordinary person, and there can have been few of these'.

96. According to N. Schmidt, here again the speaker in the song is not an individual, but the people. But all the Job poetry is primarily concerned with the fate of the individual. Verse 2b would be quite unthinkable in that case, and the wording of vv. 1a and 5f. also tells against the assumption.

97. So also v. Orelli, Giesebrecht, Rothstein; cf. also Caspari, pp. 845ff., who does not, however, express his view clearly.

98. So also Caspari, pp. 847f.

99. An 'inverted' pentameter with the scheme 2 + 3; cf. Ed. Sievers, *Metrische Studien*, I (1901), pp. 111f. Similarly 23.9b.

100. There is of course no connection with the proclamation of distress (15.5-9) which precedes; there is no point in trying to understand 15.10 in this way (Caspari, p. 855).

101. So already Ewald, Graf, Keil; most recently also Caspari, pp. 853f.

102. Duhm and Erbt resort to drastic emendations of the text, Cornill and H. Schmidt give the verse up as hopelessly corrupt, Giesebrecht and Rothstein delete it.

103. So, de Dieu and Umbreit, cf. Graf, *ad loc.*

104. Cf. H. Winckler, *Vorderasien im zweiten Jahrtausend* [The Near East in the Second Millennium] (1913), p. 61.

105. Contrast Goethe:

> pillars, columns one may break,
> > but not a free heart.
> > (*Des Epimenides Erwachen*, Act 2, Scene 6).

106. Cf. above, pp. 68f.

107. Cf. above, p. 30.

108. Naturally, one has to grant (Caspari, p. 860 n. 1), that אמר occurs now and then in the prophets too. But Hölscher has correctly seen that in the present form and in a context such as this it is 'psalmistic'. Even though the

accents seem to have taken ואמרתי as a *perfectum consecutivum*, thus frequentative (Gesenius-Kautzsch, §112kk), this hardly precludes a comparison with the other passages; and the accentuation may not even be original.

109. When N. Schmidt vocalizes אזכרנו as a hiphil and relates it to the liturgical calling upon Yahweh, this of course is dependent on his also seeing this song as spoken by the people; this is ruled out in any case by vv. 7a and 9a.

110. Similarly Caspari, p. 860: 'Perhaps the first two sentences (of 20.9) only mean that the speaker finds it painful to do without his access to Yahweh via the cult'.

111. Giesebrecht suggests reading this as בְּעָצְמָתִי 'with all my strength'!

112. Cf. also Hölscher, p. 32.

113. Cf. Gunkel, *Ausgewählte Psalmen* (3rd edn), p. 141.

114. For vv. 17f. one is tempted to posit two tristichs (3 + 3 + 3); but it is more likely to be a case of a 'mixed group' (*Mischgruppe*) to use Sievers' term, i.e. the link of the simple 'series' (*Reihe*) (3) with the 'period' (*Periode*) (3 + 3), cf. Sievers, *Metrische Studien*, I (1901), pp. 123ff.

115. Cf. Job 3; 10.18f.; *4 Ezra* 5.45. Popular belief appears to accept the possibility of eternal pregnancy (v. 17), e.g. as the result of a curse; cf. E. Sklarek, *Ungarische Volksmärchen* [Hungarian Folk-Tales] (1901), pp. 57ff.; *Anmerkungen zu den Kinder- und Hausmärchen der Brüder Grimm* [Notes on the Grimm Brothers' children's and family fairy-tales], revised edition by J. Bolte and G. Polivka, II (1915), pp. 246f.

116. Caspari (p. 859) thinks of Jeremiah's stay in the cistern (ch. 38): 'One has the impression that his constitution suffered a shock at that time which it never got over'. However, the reference can hardly be to physical suffering!

117. So, Budde, *Hiob* [Job] (2nd edn, 1913), p. 11; Cornill, *Jeremia*, p. 239; Duhm, *Hiob* (1897), p. 17; *Jeremia*, p. 166; Erbt, p. 188; Giesebrecht, *Jeremia* (2nd edn), p. 116; Graf, p. 282; Steuernagel, in Kautzsch (3rd edn), II, p. 300. A different view is held by Dillmann, *Hiob* (4th edn, 1891), p. xxxiii; N. Schmidt *Encycl. Bibl.*, II, p. 2389; previously, with some hesitation, Hitzig, *Jeremia*, p. 159.

*Notes to Chapter 4*

1. Cf. e.g. Stade, *Bibl. Theologie*, I (1905), p. 328.

2. Cf. Budde, *ZAW* 2 (1882), pp. 1-52. [This is now of course over 100 years ago!—Tr.]

3. Cf. Gunkel, *Die israelitische Literatur*, pp. 86ff.; in the introduction to H. Schmidt, pp. lviiiff.

4. Cf. above, p. 59.

5. Cf. above, p. 36.

6. Cf. above, pp. 48 and 53ff.

7. Cf. above, p. 77.

8. The extent to which they agree in the poet's personality will be discussed later (pp. 87f.).

9. I delete לבי, and instead take up נפשי from the following line (G).

10. מבלי גהה (Graf, Giesebrecht).

11. I vocalize the first עלי in accordance with the second, deleting the latter.

12. Erbt has a new poem begin at v. 20; but cf. H. Schmidt, p. 238.

13. השברתי is a gloss (G).

14. כי is to be deleted (G).

15. ואני אמרתי is an explanatory addition (Erbt, Rothstein).

16. With STV read חֶלְיִי (Hitzig, Giesebrecht, Cornill, Rothstein).

17. The opening words and רמע תרמע are to be deleted. Since there is no connection with the preceding verses (Duhm; Erbt, pp. 216f.; H. Schmidt, p. 258), the second-person plural suffixes should of course not, with G, be inserted (against BH).

18. גוה without suffix is odd—perhaps יָגוֹן should be read (Ehrlich).

19. בתולת is to be deleted.

20. Read מכתה (Ehrlich).

21. I read חוֹלְאֵי (cf. H. Schmidt, p. 257). Verse 18b anyway does not belong in this context, even if it is authentic (Cornill, H. Schmidt).

22. Read עכרו (Ehrlich).

23. An 'inverted' pentameter as in 15.12; cf. above, ch. 3 n. 99.

24. Cf. Erbt, p. 184.

25. Chapter 45 was disputed by Reuss and later by Schwally (*ZAW* 8 [1888], p. 217); cf. Duhm. On the other hand the authenticity of 16.19f., where, in v. 19a, the trust motif is present, is extremely doubtful. Since these verses interrupt the context between v. 18 and v. 21 and seem also to belong to a later period as far as content is concerned, they should be deleted (Cornill; Duhm; Hölscher, p. 399; Mowinckel, p. 50; H. Schmidt, p. 256; *et al.*).

26. See above, p. 16.

27. Cf. also the songs discussed above, pp. 83ff.

28. Cf. above, p. 19; Balla, pp. 67ff.

29. Mowinckel (pp. 22f.) has recently demonstrated that 14.1–15.4 should not be taken as originally a unity, a grand liturgy with a dialogue between Yahweh and prophet, as the redactor evidently understood it to be.

30. In v. 10b, the mention of 'Yahweh' in the third person is noticeable but rather than delete this half of the verse accordingly, with most recent scholars, it is sufficient to cancel the words ויהוה לא רצם and read אזכר and אפקד (Budde).

31. Stade, Duhm, Erbt, Cornill, Hölscher.
32. Cf. above, pp. 83f.
33. Cf. the commentaries, Erbt, p. 211; Mowinckel, p. 50.
34. Cf. above, ch. 3 n. 76.
35. Like most of the prophets Jeremiah too alluded to or made use of the *dirge* (cf. Budde, *ZAW* 2 [1882], pp. 22ff.), namely in 6.26; 7.29; 9.9, 16-21. This is, however, to be sharply distinguished from the song of lament, even if there are occasional points of contact—compare 9.17b with 8.23 and 14.17, on one hand, with Lam. 1.16; 2.11 on the other: the weeping has a rightful location in both places. However, it is easy for elements of the song of lament to intrude in the dirge, which is figurative of cases of national distress; cf. Lam. 1.12-16, 18-22.
36. Gunkel, *Die israelitische Literatur*, p. 89; *RGG*, IV, col. 1942.
37. In comparison, one might refer to the 'formulae' in the Homeric epics, on which cf. E. Drerup, *Homer* (2nd edn, 1915), pp. 33ff.
38. Cf. above, pp. 39f.
39. For examples, see Gunkel in H. Schmidt, pp. lix ff.
40. Cf. e.g. Budde, *Geschichte der althebräischen Literatur* [History of Ancient Hebrew Literature] (1906), pp. 261ff.; Kittel, *PRE*, XVI, pp. 203ff.
41. Cf. Gunkel in *RGG*, IV, cols. 1940ff., 1951.
42. For other psalm types we have a greater amount of more compelling evidence. The outline of the hymn, for example, is found already in the song of Miriam (Exod. 15.21). Further arguments are presented in Gunkel's article mentioned in the previous note.
43. Cf. H. Zimmern, *Babylonische Hymnen und Gebete* [Babylonian Hymns and Prayers], I (1905), II (1911); O. Weber, *Die Literatur der Babylonier und Assyrer* (1907), pp. 133-47; M. Jastrow, *Die Religion Babyloniens und Assyriens*, II (1912), pp. 1-137; A. Ungnad in Gressmann, *Altorientalische Texte und Bilder* [Ancient Oriental Texts and Pictures], I (1909), pp. 85-93; P. Jensen, *Texte zur assyrisch-babylonischen Religion* (= *Keilinschriftliche Bibliothek*, VI 2 [1915]); a comparison with Israelite songs of lament is made by Balla, pp. 76-88.
44. Cf. Jensen, pp. 124ff.; Gressmann, pp. 85ff.; Zimmern, I, pp. 19ff.
45. Cf. above, p. 52.
46. Jastrow, II, p. 33.
47. E.g. in the aforementioned song to Ishtar, ll. 56, 59, 93.
48. Jastrow, I, p. 310.
49. Jastrow, II, pp. 69, 76, 77, 85, 86, 89, 96, 110, 135.
50. Jensen, pp. 166ff.; Jastrow, II, pp. 72, 76, 86, 89, 102f.
51. E.g. ll. 23-32 in the 'song of the suffering righteous man' (Jensen pp. 183ff.; Gressmann, pp. 92f.; Jastrow II, pp. 120ff.).
52. Cf. Jensen, pp. 172ff.; Zimmern, I, pp. 25ff.; Jastrow, II, pp. 74ff.
53. Jastrow, II, pp. 65, 79.
54. Jastrow, II, pp. 9, 29, 84.

55. Jastrow, II, pp. 5, 107ff.

56. Cf. Jensen, pp. 72ff.; Jastrow II, pp. 28f., 31.

57. Zimmern, I, p. 19; Jastrow, II, pp. 106, 116f.

58. Jastrow, II, pp. 61f., 116.

59. Jastrow, II, pp. 77, 79, 115.

60. Cf. Ad. Erman, 'Denksteine aus der thebanischen Gräberstadt' [Memorial Stones from the Theban Necropolis], *Sitzungsberichte d. Kgl. Preuss. Akademie d. Wissenschaften*, 49 (1911), pp. 1086ff.; followed by Gunkel, *Reden und Aufsätze* [Talks and Essays] (1913), pp. 141ff. and Balla, pp. 93ff.

61. Erman, pp. 1094f.; Gunkel, p. 143.

62. Not part of the song itself, but signifying that direct speech follows.

63. Erman, pp. 1001f.

64. Cf. S. Landersdorfer, *Eine babylonische Quelle für das Buch Job?* [A Babylonian Source for the Book of Job?] (1911), pp. 79f.

65. Cf. Gunkel, *Reden und Aufsätze*, pp. 97, 110; Kittel, *Die Psalmen*, p. xxxii.

66. One should not forget, of course, that conditions will have been considerably simpler in Canaan than in Babylonia and Assyria. Thus only the larger Canaanite and Israelite sanctuaries can be considered as possible sites for such an educated cult.

67. Gunkel, in H. Schmidt, p. lxiv. Caspari (pp. 850f.) rightly reminds us that as the offspring of an ancient priestly family, he must have been particularly acquainted and familiar with cultic poetry. It is hardly legitimate, though, to speak of 'priestly devotional literature'; nor is it likely that he himself was the first to create the 'spiritual' out of the cultic song.

68. Reading אבים (Smit, K. Marti, *Das Dodekapropheton* [1904], *ad loc.*, BH following ST).

69. I read יִשָּׁאֶה for ישא and delete ויהי ריב as a variant of what follows (Gunkel).

70. לנצח is to be deleted.

71. I delete יצא (BH) and place the article before the second משפט.

72. Cf. Marti; Hölscher, pp. 442f.

73. Cf. above, p. 75.

74. Cf. Budde, *Die altisraelitische Religion* (3rd edn, 1912), p. 147 n. 12.

75. Cf. Hölscher, pp. 148f.

76. So, for example, Cornill, *Zur Einleitung in das AT* (1912), p. 108.

77. Since the literary types of the Old Testament are forms that are used with some freedom, it is better to avoid the word 'schema' altogether.

78. *Zur Einleitung in das AT* (1912), p. 84.

# INDEX TO PROPHETIC PASSAGES DISCUSSED